BRITISH R~~A~~

LOC

THIRTY-EIGHTH EDITION
SPRING 1997

The Complete Guide to all
Locomotives which run on
Britain's Mainline Railways

UPDATED TO 1998 EDITION 1.1.98

Peter Fox and Richard Bolsover

ISBN 1 872524 91 5

CONTENTS

ACQUISITION OF INFORMATION

This book has been published with great difficulty. Privatisation of the railways and the splitting up of BR into different companies has been used as an excuse to deny the railway press access to official rolling stock library information, breaking a tradition of freely-supplied information which has existed for around half a century. We hope that readers will find the information accurate, but cannot be responsible for any inaccuracies.

We would like to thank the companies and individuals which have been co-operative in supplying information and would ask other companies which find this book useful to help us in future to make the book as accurate as possible.

This book is updated to 15th November 1996..

ORGANISATION OF BRITAIN'S RAILWAY SYSTEM.

INFRASTRUCTURE

Britains state-owned railway infrastructure, i.e. the track, signalling, stations and overhead line equipment is now owned by a new company known as ''Railtrack''. This has recently been privatised. Many stations and maintenance depots are leased to train operating companies.

OPERATIONS

Passenger trains are operated by train operating companies (TOCs). A number of these have now been franchised and the rest of the franchises will shortly be let. The following TOCs are now franchised:

InterCity East Coast (Now renamed Great North Eastern Railway (GNER). Owned by Sea Containers Ltd.

Midland Mainline and Gatwick Express. Owned by National Express Group.

Network South Central and South Eastern Trains (Now renamed Connex South Central and Connex South Eastern). Owned by Société Générale des Entreprises Automobiles, a subsidiary of Compagnie Générale des Eaux.

South West Trains and Island Line. Owned by Stagecoach UK.

Great Western Trains. Joint management buy-out with British Bus.

Chiltern Railways. Owned by M40 Trains, a management buy-out.

London Tilbury & Southend, South Wales & West and Cardiff Railway Company. Owned by Prism, a company whose principal shareholder is East Yorkshire Motor Services. Prism has also been named as preferred bidder for West Anglia Great Northern.

Thames Trains. Owned by Victory Railway Holdings, a joint venture between the Go Ahead group and Thames Trains management.

As we went to press, it was announced that the Virgin group was the preferred bidder for Cross Country Trains, FirstBus was the preferred bidder for Great Eastern and GB Railways was the preferred bidder for Anglia.

Eurostar trains are operated by Eurostar (UK) Ltd. jointly with French Railways (SNCF) and Belgian Railways (NMBS/SNCB). Eurostar (UK) will also operate the Night Service trains jointly with SNCF, Netherlands Railways (NS) and German Railways (DB).

Rail Express Systems, which operated mail and charter trains, together with trainload freight companies LoadHaul, Mainline and TransRail have been bought by the North & South Railway Company whose main shareholder is Wisconsin Central Transportation Corporation of the USA. The four concerns have been combined and now known as the English, Welsh and Scottish Railway Ltd. (EWS or EW&S). TOPS pool codes are still based on the former four companies, but this is expected to change before long.

Container trains are operated by Freightliner which has been sold to a management buyout and general freight, particularly Channel Tunnel traffic is handled by Railfreight Distribution (RfD) which is at a late stage in the privatisation process. Certain other companies e.g. National Power operate freight trains with their own locomotives.

OWNERSHIP OF LOCOMOTIVES AND ROLLING STOCK

The locomotives of EWS and those of Eurostar are owned by those companies. Most locomotives, hauled coaching stock and multiple unit vehicles used by the passenger train operating companies are owned by three leasing companies which were originally set up by British Railways as subsidiaries and then privatised. These are:

Eversholt Holdings (formerly Eversholt Leasing)
Angel Trains
Porterbrook Leasing Company Ltd.

Other vehicles are owned by various private companies such as The Carriage and Traction Co. Ltd., Carnforth Railway Restoration & Engineering Serv ices Ltd., Titanstar Ltd. and the Venice Simplon-Orient Express Ltd.

Further details of these companies will be found in the section on abbreviations and codes. Thus for each vehicle it is generally necessary to specify both the owner and the TOC which currently operates the vehicle.

Finally, a number of 'service' type vehicles are owned by Railtrack (e.g. Sandite vehicles) and others are owned by former BR Headquarters organisations which have now been privatised e.g. Railtest or by railway vehicle manufacturing and repair companies. Royal Train vehicles are owned by Railtrack.

In this book, ownng companies are detailed in the information section at the head of each class. EWS and Eurostar locos are assumed to be owned by that company, as are shunters belonging to privatised train operating companies.

INTRODUCTION

The following notes are applicable to locomotives:

DETAILS & DIMENSIONS

Principal details and dimensions are given for each class in metric units. Imperial equivalents are also given for power. Maximum speeds are still quoted in miles per hour since imperial units are still used in day to day railway operations in Britain.. Since the present maximum permissible speed of certain classes of locomotives is different from the design speed, these are now shown separately in class details. In some cases certain low speed limits are arbitrary and may occasionally be raised when necessary if a locomotive has to be pressed into passenger service.

LOCOMOTIVE DETAIL DIFFERENCES

Detail differences which affect the areas and types of train which locos work are shown. Where detail differences occur within a class or part class of locomotives., these are shown against the individual locomotive number. Except where shown, diesel locomotives have no train heating equipment. Electric or electro-diesel locomotives are assumed to have train heating unless shown otherwise. Standard abbreviations used are:

a	Train air brakes only.
c	Fitted with Scharfenberg couplers for Eurostar working.
e	Fitted with electric heating apparatus (ETH).
j	Fitted with RCH jumper cables for operating with PCVs (propelling control vehicles)
r	Fitted with radio electronic token block equipment.
s	Slow speed control fitted (and operable).
t	Fitted with automatic vehicle identification transponders.
v	Train vacuum brakes only.
x	Dual train brakes (air & vacuum).
y	ETH equipped but equipment isolated.
+	Extended range locos with Additional fuel tank capacity compared with others in class.

After the locomotive number are shown any notes regarding braking, heating etc., the livery code (in bold type), the pool code where applicable, the depot code and name if any. Locomotives which have been renumbered in recent years show the last number in parentheses after the current number. For previous numbers of other locos, please refer to the Platform 5 Book ''Diesel & Electric Loco. Register''

NAMES

All official names are shown as they appear on the locomotive i.e. all upper case or upper & lower case lettering. Where only a few locomotives in a class are named, these are shown in a separate table at the end of the class or sub-class.

DEPOT ALLOCATIONS & POOL CODES

The depot at which a locomotive is allocated is the one at which it receives its main examinations. This depot may be a long way away from where it normally performs its duties. The pool code is a better means of ascertaining where a locomotive may operate, but it should be borne in mind that often locomotives of the same company may be used in pools other than their official pool.In addition, English Welsh & Scottish Railway are likely to move towards a common user system in future. (S) denotes stored serviceable and (U) stored unserviceable. Locos may not be stored at their home depots. Thus the layout is as follows:

No.	Old No.	Notes	Liv.	Pool	Depot	Name
47777	(47636)		**RX**	PXLB	CD	Restored

GENERAL INFORMATION ON BRITISH RAILWAYS' LOCOMOTIVES

CLASSIFICATION & NUMBERING

Initially BR diesel locomotives were allocated numbers in the 1xxxx series, with electrics allotted numbers in the 2xxxx series. Around 1957 diesel locomotives were allocated new numbers with between one and four digits with 'D' prefixes. Diesel electric shunters in the 13xxx series had the '1' replaced by a 'D', but diesel mechanical shunters were completely renumbered. Electric locomotives retained their previous numbers but with an 'E' prefix.

When all standard gauge steam locomotives had been withdrawn, the prefix letter was removed. In 1972, the present TOPS numbering system was introduced whereby the loco number consisted of a two-digit class number followed by a serial number. In some cases the last two digits of the former number were generally retained (Classes 20, 37, 50), but in other classes this is not the case. In this book former TOPS numbers carried byrecently- converted locos. are shown in parentheses. Full renumbering informaton is to be found in the 'Diesel & Electric loco Register', the new third edition of which is now available.

Diesel locomotives are classified as "types" depending on their engine horsepower as follows:

Type	Engine hp.	Old Number Range	Current Classes
1	800-1000	D 8000-D 8999	20.
2	1001-1499	D 5000-D 6499/D 7500-D 7999	31.
3	1500-1999	D 6500-D 7499	33, 37.
4	2000-2999	D 1-D 1999	46, 47.
5	3000+	D 9000-D 9499	55, 56, 58, 59, 60.
Shunter	300-799	D 3000-D 4999	08, 09.

Class 14 (650 hp diesel hydraulics) were numbered in the D95xx series.

Electric and electro-diesel locomotives are classified according to their supply system. Locomotives operating on a d.c. system are allocated classes 71-80, whilst a.c. or dual voltage locomotives start at Class 81. Departmental locomotives which remain self propelled or which are likely to move around on a day to day basis are classified Class 97.

WHEEL ARRANGEMENT

For main line diesel and electric locomotives the system whereby the number of driven axles on a bogie or frame is denoted by a letter (A = 1, B = 2, C = 3 etc.) and the number of undriven axles is noted by a number is used. The letter 'o' after a letter indicates that each axle is individually powered and a + sign indicates that the bogies are intercoupled. For shunters the Whyte notation is used. In this notation, generally used in Britain for steam locomotives, the number of leading wheels are given, followed by the number of driving wheels and then the trailing wheels.

HAULING CAPABILITY OF DIESEL LOCOS

The hauling capability of a diesel locomotive depends basically upon three factors:

1. Its adhesive weight. The greater the weight on its driving wheels, the greater the adhesion and thus more tractive power can be applied before wheel slip occurs.

2. The characteristics of its transmission. In order to start a train the locomotive has to exert a pull at standstill. A direct drive diesel engine cannot do this, hence the need for transmission. This may be mechanical, hydraulic or electric. The current British standard for locomotives is electric transmission. Here the diesel engine drives a generator or alternator and the current produced is fed to the traction motors. The force produced by each driven wheel depends on the current in its traction motor. In other words the larger the current, the harder it pulls.

As the locomotive speed increases, the current in the traction motors falls hence the *Maximum Tractive Effort* is the maximum force at its wheels that the locomotive can exert at a standstill. The electrical equipment cannot take such high currents for long without overheating. Hence the *Continuous Tractive Effort* is quoted which represents the current which the equipment can take continuously.

3. The power of its engine. Not all of this power reaches the rail as electrical machines are approximately 90% efficient. As the electrical energy passes through two such machines (the generator/alternator and the traction motors), the *Power At Rail* is about 81% (90% of 90%) of the engine power, less a further amount used for auxiliary equipment such as radiator fans, traction motor cooling fans, air compressors, battery charging, cab heating, ETH, etc. The power of the locomotive is proportional to the tractive effort times the speed. Hence when on full power there is a speed corresponding to the continuous tractive effort.

HAULING CAPABILITY OF ELECTRIC LOCOS

Unlike a diesel locomotive, an electric locomotive does not develop its power on board and its performance is determined only by two factors, namely its weight and the characteristics of its electrical equipment. Whereas a diesel locomotive tends to be a constant power machine, the power of an electric locomotive varies considerably. Up to a certain speed it can produce virtually a constant tractive effort. Hence power rises with speed according to the formula given in section 3 above, until a maximum speed is reached at which tractive effort falls, such that the power also falls. Hence the power at the speed corresponding to the maximum tractive effort is lower than the maximum.

BRAKE FORCE

The brake force is a measure of the braking power of a locomotive. This is shown on the locomotive data panels so that railway staff can ensure that sufficient brake power is available on freight trains.

TRAIN HEATING AND POWER EQUIPMENT

The standard system in use in Britain for heating loco hauled trains is by means of electricity and is now known as ETS (Electric train supply). Locomotives which were equipped to provide steam heating have had this equipment removed or rendered inoperable (isolated). Electric heat is provided from the locomotive by means of a separate alternator on the loco, except in the case of Class 33 which have a d.c. generator. The *ETH Index* is a measure of the electrical power available for train heating. All electrically heated coaches have an ETH index and the total of these in a train must not exceed the ETH power of a locomotive.

ROUTE AVAILABILITY

This is a measure of a railway vehicle's axle load. The higher the axle load of a vehicle, the higher the RA number on a scale 1 to 10. Each route on BR has an RA number and in theory no vehicle with a higher RA number may travel on that route without special clearance. Exceptions are made, however.

MULTIPLE AND PUSH-PULL WORKING

Multiple working between diesel locomotives in Britain has usually been provided by means of an electro-pneumatic system, with special jumper cables connecting the locos. A coloured symbol is painted on the end of the locomotive to denote which system is in use. Class 47s nos. 47701-17 used a time-division multiplex (t.d.m.) system which utilised the existing RCH (an abbreviation for the former railway clearing house, a pre-nationalisation standards organisation) jumper cables for push-pull working. These had in the past only been used for train lighting control, and more recently for public address (pa) and driver-guard communication. A new standard t.d.m. system is now fitted to all a.c. electric locomotives and other vehicles, enabling them to work in both push-pull and multiple working modes. RfD and Freightliner 1995 Ltd. Class 47 locomotives are now being fitted with a 'green circle' multiple working system.. Full details of the mechanism of this new multiple-working system is not to hand.

1. DIESEL LOCOMOTIVES

CLASS 08   BR SHUNTER   0-6-0

Built: 1953–62 by BR at Crewe, Darlington, Derby, Doncaster or Horwich Works.
Engine: English Electric 6KT of 298 kW (400 hp) at 680 rpm.
Main Generator: English Electric 801.
Traction Motors: Two English Electric 506.
Max. Tractive Effort: 156 kN (35000 lbf).
Cont. Tractive Effort: 49 kN (11100 lbf) at 8.8 m.p.h.

Power At Rail: 194 kW (260 hp).	**Length over Buffers:** 8.92 m.
Brake Force: 19 t.	**Wheel Diameter:** 1372 mm.
Design Speed: 20 m.p.h.	**Weight:** 50 t.
Max. Speed: 15 or 20* m.p.h.	**RA:** 5.

Non-standard liveries:

08296, 08602, 08846 and 08943 are grey and carry numbers 001, D 3769, D 4144 and 002 respectively.

08414 is 'D' with RfD brandings and also carries its former number D 3529.

08460 is light grey with a dark grey roof, black cab doors and window surrounds and 'TLF South East' branding.

08500 is red lined out in black & white.

08519 is BR black.

08527 is light grey with a black roof, blue bodyside stripe and 'Ilford Level 5' branding.

08593 is Great Eastern blue lined out in red and also carries its former number D 3760.

08601 is London Midland & Scottish Railway black.

08629 is Royal purple.

08642 is London & South Western Railway black and also carries its former number D 3809.

08649 is grey with blue, white and red stripes and 'WTL' branding. Carries its original number D 3816.

08689 is 'D' with Railfreight general markings.

08699 is grey and carries no number.

08715 is in experimental dayglo orange livery.

08721 is blue with a red & yellow stripe ('Red Star' livery).

08730 is BR black.

08805 is LMS maroon and also carries its former number 3973.

08867 is BR black.

08879 is turquoise with full yellow ends, black cab doors, black numbers on a yellow background and RfD brandings.

08883 is Caledonian blue.

08907 is London & North Western Railway black.

08938 is grey and red.

08616 carries its former number D 3783. 08830 is on long-term lease to the East Somerset Railway.

n – Waterproofed for working at Oxley Carriage Depot.
z – Fitted with buckeye adaptor at nose end for HST depot shunting.
§ – Fitted with yellow flashing light and siren for working between Ipswich Yard and Cliff Quay.
Originally numbered in series D 3000 – 4192.

Note: All DFLS locos are owned by Porterbrook Leasing Company.

CLASS 08/0. Standard Design.

08296	v	**0**		ZC	08514	a		FDSD	DR
08388	a	**FP**	FDSX	IM (U)	08516	a	**D**	FDSK	KY
08389	a		DAWE	AN	08517	a		EWSX	SF (S)
08393	a	**D**	DAWE	AN	08519	a	**0**	LCWX	BS (U)
08397	a	**F**	LWSP	SP	08523	x	**ML**	EWOC	OC
08401	a	**D**	FDSI	IM	08525	x	**F**	HISL	NL
08402	a	**D**	PXLT	CD	08526	x		EWOC	OC
08405	a	**D**	FDSI	IM	08527	x	**0**		ZI
08410	a	**D**	HJXX	PM	08528	x	**D**	ENSN	TO
08411	a		LGML	ML	08529	x		ENSN	TO
08413	a	**D**	DASY	TI	08530	x	**D**	DFLS	SF
08414	a*§	**0**	EWSX	SF	08531	x	**D**	DFLS	SF
08417	a		CDJD	DY	08534	x	**D**	LGML	ML
08418	a	**F**	FDSD	DR	08535	x	**D**	DASY	TI
08428	a		LCWX	BS (U)	08536	x		HISE	DY
08441	a		ENSN	TO	08538	x	**D**	ENSN	TO
08442	a	**F**	FDSX	KY	08540	x	**D**	ENZX	TO (U)
08445	a		FDSX	IM (U)	08541	x	**D**	EWSF	SF
08448	a		LCXX	BS (U)	08542	x	**F**	EWSX	SF
08449	a		ENXX	TO (U)	08543	x	**D**	LBBS	BS
08451	x		HFSN	WN	08561	x		LGML	ML
08454	x		HFSN	WN	08567	x		LBBS	BS
08460	a	**0**	EWSX	SF	08568	x			ZH
08466	a	**F0**	FDSX	IM (U)	08569	x		DAAN	AN
08472	a		HBSH	BN	08571	xz		HBSH	EC
08480	az	**G**	EWOC	OC	08573	x			ZI
08481	x		LNCF	CF	08575	x	**BS**	DFLS	TI
08482	a	**D**	DAWE	AN	08576	x		LNCF	CF
08483	a	**D**	HJXX	PM	08577	x		FMSY	TE
08484	a	**D**		ZN	08578	x	**R**	PXLS	HT
08485	a		LWSP	SP	08580	x		ENSN	TO
08489	a	**F**	LWSP	SP	08581	x	**BS**	FDSX	DR (S)
08492	a		ENSN	TO	08582	a	**D**	FMSY	TE
08493	a		LNCF	CF	08585	x		DFLS	CD
08495	x		ENSN	TO	08586	a	**F**	LCXX	AY (U)
08499	a	**F**	FDSK	KY	08587	x		FDSD	DR
08500	x	**0**	FDSD	DR	08588	xz	**BS**	HISL	NL
08506	a		LGML	ML	08593	x	**0**	EWSF	SF
08509	a	**F**	FDSD	DR	08594	x		PXLT	CD (U)
08510	a		FDSD	DR	08597	x		ENZX	TO
08511	a		ENSN	TO	08599	x		PXLS	CD
08512	a	**F**	FDSD	DR	08600	a	**D**	EWSX	SF

No.				
08601	x	0	LBBS	BS
08602	x	0		ZD
08605	x		FDSK	KY
08607	x		ENXX	TO (U)
08610	x		LCXX	BS (U)
08611	x		HFSL	LO
08616	x	G	HGSS	TS
08617	x		HFSN	WN
08619	x		LCXX	SP (S)
08622	x		LCWX	ML (U)
08623	x		LBBS	BS
08624	x		DFLS	CD
08625	x		LBBS	BS
08628	x		LBBS	BS
08629	x	0		ZN
08630	x		LGML	ML
08632	x		FDSI	IM
08633	x	RX	PXLS	CD
08635	x		PXLS	CD
08641	xz	D	HJSL	LA
08642	x*	0	DFLS	EH
08643	xz	D	HJXX	PM
08644	xz	I	HJSL	LA
08645	xz	D	HJSL	LA
08646	x	F	EWOC	OC
08647	x	G	PXXA	CD
08648	x*	D	HJSL	LA
08649	x	0		ZG
08651	xz	D	EWOC	OC
08653	x*	FE	DAAN	AN
08655	x*	F	DAWE	AN
08661	a	FE	DAYX	AN (U)
08662	x		FDSK	KY
08663	a	D	HJSL	LA
08664	x		EWOC	OC
08665	x		FDSI	IM
08668	x		PXXA	CD
08670	a		EWSX	SF
08675	x	F	LGML	ML
08676	x		LWSP	SP
08682	x			ZF
08683	x		LBBS	BS
08685	x		PXLS	CD
08689	a	0	EWSX	SF
08690	x		HISE	DY
08691	x	G	DFLS	CD
08692	x	0		ZC (U)
08693	x		LCWX	ML (U)
08694	x		DASY	TI
08695	x		PXLT	CD
08696	a	D	HFSN	WN
08697	x		HISE	DY
08698	a		EWSU	SU
08699	x			ZC
08700	a		EWSX	SF (S)
08701	x	RX	PXLS	CD
08702	x		PXLS	WN
08703	a		DAAN	AN
08706	x		FDSK	KY
08709	x		EWOC	OC
08711	x	RX	PXLS	CD
08713	a		FDSX	DR (U)
08714	x	RX	PXLS	CD
08715	v	0	EWSX	SF
08718	x		LCWX	ML (U)
08720	a	D	LGML	ML
08721	x	0	HFSL	LO
08723	x		ENXX	TO (U)
08724	x		HBSH	BN
08730	x	0		ZH
08731	x		LCWX	ML (U)
08734	x		LCWX	BS (U)
08735	x		LGML	ML
08737	x	FE	DAWE	AN
08738	x	D	LGML	ML
08739	x		DAAN	AN
08740	x	F	EWSX	SF
08742	x	RX	PXLS	CD
08745	xz	FE	DFLS	CD
08746	x	D	LBBS	BS
08750	x		EWSF	SF
08751	x	FE	DASY	TI
08752	x	C	EWSF	SF
08754	x		HASS	IS
08756	x	D	LNCF	CF
08757	x	RX	PXLS	HT
08758	x		EWSX	SF
08762	x		HASS	IS
08765	xn	D	LBBS	BS
08768	x		LGML	ML
08770	a	D	LNCF	CF
08773	x		ENXX	TO (U)
08775	x		EWSF	SF
08776	a	D	FDSK	KY
08780	x		HJSE	LE
08782	a		FDSK	KY
08783	x		FDSK	KY
08784	x		DAAN	AN
08786	a	D	LNCF	CF
08790	x		HFSL	LO
08792	x		LNWK	CF
08795	x	M	HJSE	LE

No.			Code	
08798	x		LNCF	CF
08799	x		DAAN	AN
08801	x		LNCF	CF
08802	x	RX	PXLS	CD
08804	x		PXLS	CD (S)
08805	x	O	HGSS	TS
08806	a	F	FMSY	TE
08807	x	BS	LBBS	BS
08810	a		HSSN	NC
08811	a*		EWSX	SF (S)
08813	a	D	FMSY	TE
08815	x		LCWX	SP (U)
08817	x	BS	LWSP	SP
08818	x		PXXA	CD
08819	x	D	LNCF	CF
08822	x	M	HJSE	LE
08823	a			ZF
08824	a	F	FDSI	IM
08825	a		DAAN	AN
08826	a		LCWX	ML (U)
08827	a		LGML	ML
08828	a		EWSX	SF
08830	x*		HLSV	CF
08834	x	FD	HBSH	BN
08836	x	I	HJXX	OO
08837	x*	D	DAAN	AN
08842	x		DAAN	AN
08844	x		DAWE	AN
08846	x	O		ZC
08847	x*			ZG
08853	xr		HBSH	EC
08854	x*		EWEH	EH
08856	x		DAAN	AN
08865	x		PXLT	CD
08866	x		EWSF	SF
08867	x	O	LWSP	SP
08869	x	G	HSSN	NC
08872	x	D	DAAN	AN
08873	x	RX	PXLS	CD
08877	x	D	FDSD	DR
08878	x		EWSX	SF (U)
08879	x	O	DATI	TI
08881	x	D	LGML	ML
08882	x		LGML	ML
08883	x	O	LGML	ML
08884	x		LWSP	SP
08886	x	EW	ENSN	TO
08887	x		HFSN	WN
08888	xz	EW	FDSI	IM
08890	x	D	PXLS	WN
08891	x		DFLS	AN
08892	x*	D	DFLS	EH
08893	x	D	LCXX	BS (U)
08894	x		LWSP	SP
08896	x		PXLS	CD
08897	x	D	PXLS	CD
08899	x		HISE	DY
08900	x	D	LNWK	CF
08901	xn		LCXX	BS (U)
08902	x		DAYX	AN (U)
08903	x		FDSX	DR (U)
08904	x		EWOC	OC
08905	x	FE	DASY	TI
08906	x		LGML	ML
08907	x	O	DAAN	AN
08908	xz		HISL	NL
08909	x		EWSF	SF
08910	x		LGML	ML
08911	x	D	LWSP	SP
08912	x		LGML	ML
08913	x	D	DAWE	AN
08914	x		LBBS	BS
08915	x	F	LWSP	SP
08918	x	D	LWSP	SP
08919	x	RX	PXLS	CD
08920	x	F	LBBS	BS
08921	x	EW	PXLS	CD
08922	x	D	LGML	ML
08924	x	D	EWOC	OC
08925	x		LWSP	SP
08926	x		DAYX	AN (U)
08927	x		LBBS	BS
08928	x	FR	HSSN	NC
08931	x		FDSX	TE (U)
08932	x		LNWK	CF
08933	x*	EW	EWSX	SF
08934	x		HFSN	WN
08938	xr	O	LCWX	ML (U)
08939	x	.	DAAN	AN
08940	x		EWEH	EH
08941	x		LNCF	CF
08942	x		LNWK	CF
08943	x	O		ZT
08944	x	D	EWOC	OC
08946	x	FE	DASY	TI
08947	x		EWOC	OC
08948	xc	E	GPSS	OC
08950	x	I	HISL	NL
08951	x	D	DAAN	AN
08952	x		LCWX	ML (U)
08953	x	D	LNCF	CF
08954	x	FT	LNWK	CF

08955 x		LNWK	CF	08957 x	EWSX	SF
08956 x		CDJD	DY	08958 x	EWSX	SF (U)

Names:

08578	Libert Dickinson	08714	Cambridge
08647	Crimpsall	08790	M.A. SMITH
08649	G.H. Stratton	08869	The Canary
08661	Europa	08879	Sheffield Children's Hospital
08682	Lionheart	08888	Postman's Pride
08701	The Sorter	08919	Steep Holm
08711	EAGLE C.U.R.C.	08950	Neville Hill 1st

Class 08/9. Fitted with cut-down cab and headlight for Cwmmawr branch.

08993 x	**FT**	LNWK	CF	ASHBURNHAM
08994 a	**D**	LNWK	CF	
08995 a	**FT**	LNWK	CF	KIDWELLY

CLASS 09　　　　BR SHUNTER　　　　0-6-0

Built: 1959 – 62 by BR at Darlington or Horwich Works.
Engine: English Electric 6KT of 298 kW (400 hp) at 680 rpm.
Main Generator: English Electric 801.
Traction Motors: English Electric 506.
Max. Tractive Effort: 111 kN (25000 lbf).
Cont. Tractive Effort: 39 kN (8800 lbf) at 11.6 m.p.h.
Power At Rail: 201 kW (269 hp).
Brake Force: 19 t.
Weight: 50 t.
Max. Speed: 27 m.p.h.
Train Brakes: Air & Vacuum.

Length over Buffers: 8.92 m.
Wheel Diameter: 1372 mm.
RA: 5.

Class 09/0 were originally numbered 3665 – 71, 3719 – 21, 4099 – 4114.

CLASS 09/0. Built as Class 09.

09001		LNCF	CF	09014	**D**	FDSK	KY
09003		EWHG	SL	09015	**D**	LNCF	CF
09004		HWSU	SU	09016	**D**	EWOC	OC
09005	**D**	FMSY	TE	09018	**ML**	EWOC	OC
09006	**ML**	EWOC	OC	09019	**ML**	EWHG	SL
09007	**ML**	EWOC	OC	09020		EWSF	SF
09008	**D**	LNCF	CF	09021	**FE**	DAWE	AN
09009	**EW**	EWHG	SL	09022		DAYX	AN
09010	**D**	EWSF	SF	09023		EWSU	SU
09011	**D**	DAWE	AN	09024	**ML**	EWHG	SL
09012	**D**	EWOC	OC	09025		HWSU	SU
09013	**D**	LNCF	CF	09026	**D**	HWSU	SU

Names:

09009	Three Bridges C.E.D.	09026	William Pearson
09012	Dick Hardy		

CLASS 09/1. Converted from Class 08. 110 V electrical equipment.

09101	D	EWOC	OC	09105	D	LNCF	CF
09102	D	EWOC	OC	09106	D	FMSY	TE
09103	D	LGML	ML	09107	D	LNCF	CF
09104	D	LBBS	BS				

CLASS 09/2. Converted from Class 08. 90 V electrical equipment.

09201	D	ENSN	TO	09204	D	FMSY	TE
09202	D	LGML	ML	09205	D	LGML	ML
09203	D	LNCF	CF				

CLASS 20   ENGLISH ELECTRIC TYPE 1   Bo–Bo

Built: 1957 – 68 by English Electric Company at Vulcan Foundry, Newton le Willows or Robert Stephenson & Hawthorn, Darlington. 20001 – 128 were originally built with disc indicators whilst 20129 – 228 were built with four character headcode panels.
Engine: English Electric 8SVT Mk. II of 746 kW (1000 hp) at 850 rpm.
Main Generator: English Electric 819/3C.
Traction Motors: English Electric 526/5D (20001 – 48) or 526/8D (others).
Max. Tractive Effort: 187 kN (42000 lbf).
Cont. Tractive Effort: 111 kN (25000 lbf) at 11 m.p.h.
Power At Rail: 574 kW (770 hp).   **Length over Buffers:** 14.25 m.
Brake Force: 35 t.   **Wheel Diameter:** 1092 mm.
Design Speed: 75 m.p.h.   **Weight:** 73.5 t.
Max. Speed: 60 m.p.h.   **RA:** 5.
Train Brakes: Air & Vacuum.
Multiple Working: Blue Star Coupling Code (Class 20/3 have non-standard jumpers).

Originally numbered in series D 8007 – 8190, D 8315 – 8325.

CLASS 20/0. EWS or Racal-BRT owned Locomotives.

Note: The Racal-BRT locomotives in traffic are operated by EWS.

20007	st		TAKX	CE (U)	
20016	st		LCXX	BS (U)	
20032	s		TAKX	CE	
20057	st		LCXX	BS (U)	
20059	st	FR	LCXX	BS (U)	
20066			LCXX	BS (U)	
20072	st		TAKX	CE (U)	
20075	st	T	TAKB	BS	Sir William Cooke
20081	st		LCXX	BS (U)	
20087	st	BS	LCXX	BS (U)	
20092		CS	LCXX	BS (U)	
20104	st	FR	TAKX	CE (U)	
20117	st		TAKX	CE (U)	
20118		FR	LCWX	BS (U)	
20121	st		TAKX	CE (U)	
20128	st	T	TAKB	BS	Guglielmo Marconi

20131	st	**T**	TAKB	BS	Almon B. Strowger
20132	st	**FR**	LCWX	BS (U)	
20138		**FR**	LCWX	BS (U)	
20165		**FR**	LCWX	BS (U)	
20168	st		LCWX	BS (U)	
20169	st	**CS**	LCWX	BS (U)	
20187	st	**T**	TAKB	BS	Sir Charles Wheatstone
20190	st		TAKX	CE (U)	
20215	st	**FR**	TAKX	CE (U)	

CLASS 20/3. Owned by Direct Rail Services.

Used on radioactive waste trains between Sellafield, Barrow Docks and Drigg and chemical trains to Northwich.
All have train air brakes only and twin fuel tanks.

Non-standard Livery: Dark blue with light blue roof and green lettering.

20301 (20047)	**0**	XHSD	SD	FURNESS RAILWAY 150
20302 (20084)	**0**	XHSD	SD	
20303 (20127)	**0**	XHSD	SD	
20304 (20120)	**0**	XHSD	SD	
20305 (20095)	**0**	XHSD	SD	

CLASS 20/9. Owned by Hunslet – Barclay Ltd.

Used mainly on weedkilling trains.

Non-standard Livery: Hunslet – Barclay two-tone grey with red solebars and black lettering.

20901 (20101)	t	**0**	XYPD	ZK	NANCY
20902 (20060)		**0**	XYPD	ZK	LORNA
20903 (20083)		**0**	XYPD	ZK	ALISON
20904 (20041)		**0**	XYPD	ZK	JANIS
20905 (20225)	t	**0**	XYPD	ZK	IONA
20906 (20219)		**0**	XYPD	ZK	Kilmarnock 400

CLASS 31   BRUSH TYPE 2   A1A – A1A

Built: 1957 – 62 by Brush Traction at Loughborough.
31102/5 – 7/10/25/34/44/444/50/61 retain two headcode lights. Others have roof-mounted headcode boxes.
Engine: English Electric 12SVT of 1100 kW (1470 hp) at 850 rpm.
Main Generator: Brush TG160-48.
Traction Motors: Brush TM73-68.
Max. Tractive Effort: 160 kN (35900 lbf) (190 kN (42800 lbf)*).
Cont. Tractive Effort: 83 kN (18700 lbf) at 23.5 m.p.h. (99 kN (22250 lbf) at 19.7 m.p.h. *.)

Power At Rail: 872 kW (1170 hp).	**Length over Buffers:** 17.30 m.
Brake Force: 49 t.	**Driving Wheel Diameter:** 1092 mm.
Design Speed: 90 (80*) m.p.h.	**Centre Wheel Diameter:** 1003 mm.
Weight: 107 – 111 t.	**Train Brakes:** Air & Vacuum.
RA: 5 or 6.	**ETH Index (Class 31/4):** 66.
Max. Speed: 60 m.p.h. (90 m.p.h. 31/4).	

Multiple Working: Blue Star Coupling Code.
Communication Equipment: Cab to shore radio-telephone.

Non-standard liveries:

31116 is red, yellow, red and grey with 'Infrastructure' branding.
31413 is BR blue with yellow cabsides, a light blue stripe along the bottom of the body and a red band around the bottom of the cabs.

Originally numbered D 5520 – 5699, D 5800 – 5862 (not in order).

CLASS 31/1. Standard Design. RA5.

31102		C	LCXX	BS	31199	FC	LCWX	SP (U)
31105	*	FT	LBDB	BS	31200	FC	LCXX	SP (U)
31106	*	C	LCWX	BS (U)	31201	FC	LWNW	SP
31107		C	LCXX	BS (U)	31203	C	LWNW	SP
31110		C	LBDB	BS	31205	FR	ENXX	TO (U)
31112	*	CT	LBDB	BS	31206	C	LCWX	BS (U)
31113		C	LBDB	BS	31207	C	LWNW	SP
31116		0	ENXX	TO (U)	31219	C	ENXX	TO (U)
31119		C	LCWX	SP (S)	31224	C	LCWX	SP (S)
31125		C	LCXX	BS (U)	31229	C	LWNW	SP
31126		C	LCWX	SP (U)	31230 *	F0	ENXX	TO (U)
31128		F0	LCXX	BS (U)	31232	C	LCWX	BS (U)
31130		FC	LWNW	SP	31233	C	LWNW	SP
31132		F0	LCWX	BS (U)	31235	C	LCWX	SP (S)
31134		C	LCWX	SP (U)	31237	C	LCWX	BS (U)
31135		C	ENXX	TO (U)	31238	C	LCWX	SP (U)
31142		C	LWNW	SP	31242	C	LCWX	SP (S)
31144		C	LCWX	SP (U)	31247	FR	ENXX	TO (U)
31145		C	LCXX	SP	31248	F0	LCXX	BS (U)
31146	r	C	LBDB	BS	31250	C	ENXX	TO (U)
31147	r	C	LCWX	BS (U)	31252	F0	ENXX	TO (U)
31149		FR	ENXX	TO (U)	31255	C	LWNW	SP
31154		C	LWNW	SP	31263	C	LCXX	SP (U)
31155		FA	LCXX	BS (U)	31268	C	ENXX	TO (U)
31158		C	LCXX	BS (U)	31270	FC	LCWX	SP (S)
31160		F	LCXX	SP (U)	31271	FA	ENXX	TO (S)
31163		C	LWNW	SP	31273	C	LBDB	BS
31164		F0	LCWX	BS (U)	31275	FC	LWNW	SP
31165		G	ENXX	TO (U)	31276	FC	ENXX	TO (U)
31166	r	C	LBDB	BS	31285	C	LCWX	SP (S)
31171		F0	LCXX	BS (U)	31294	FA	ENXX	TO (U)
31174		C	LCXX	BS (U)	31301	FR	LCXX	SP (U)
31178		C	LCWX	BS (U)	31302	FP	LCWX	SP (U)
31181		C	ENXX	TO (U)	31304	FC	LCXX	SP (U)
31185		C	LWNW	SP (S)	31306	C	LWNW	SP
31186		C	ENXX	TO (U)	31308	C	ENXX	TO (S)
31187		C	ENXX	TO (U)	31312	FC	LCXX	SP (U)
31188		C	LWNW	SP	31317	F0	LCWX	BS (U)
31190		C	LCWX	SP (S)	31319	FC	LWNW	SP
31191		C	ENXX	TO (U)	31327	FR	LCWX	SP (S)

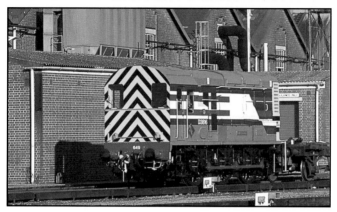

▲ Wessex Traincare liveried Class 08 No. 08649 'G.H. Stratton' is pictured at Eastleigh on 27th July 1996. This loco carries its former number D3816 *John A. Day*

▼ The first Class 09 to carry new Railfreight Distribution colours, No. 09021 is seen at Stratford Freight Terminal on 19th October 1996. *Darren Ford*

Class 20s Nos 20128 'Guglielmo Marconi' and 20075 'Sir William Cooke' approach Norton Bridge with a Crewe–Bescot ballast working on 8th May 1996. Both locos carry Racal-BR Telecom livery.
Hugh Ballantyne

▲ The sole Mainline freight liveried Class 31, No. 31407 is seen at Great Yarmouth on 31st August 1996 after arriving with the 14.35 from Norwich.   *Brian Denton*

▼ Regional Railways liveried Class 31s Nos. 31455 and 31 410 doublehead an Ince Moss to Warrington ballast at Winwick on 5th July 1996.   *Paul Senior*

▲ Civil-link liveried Class 33 No. 33051 'Shakespeare Cliff' at Hoo Junction on 10th October 1995 after arriving with a train from East Peckham tip. *Rodney Lissenden*

▼ A Fawley to Eastleigh trip working consisting of empty bogie tankers passes through Southampton on 8th February 1996 behind Mainline freight liveried Class 37 No. 37167. *Nic Joynson*

▲ English, Welsh & Scottish Railway liveried Class 37 No. 37419 is pictured near Sellafield on 24th July 1996 with a nuclear flask train working. *Dave McAlone*

▼ New Railfreight Distribution liveried Class 47 No. 47310 'Henry Ford' passes Droitwich Spa with a Washwood Heath to MoD Long Marston train on 16th October 1996. *Bob Sweet*

An HST set in the new Great Western Trains livery catches the early morning sun as it passes through Dawlish with Class 43 power cars Nos. 43183 and 43185 'Great Western' in charge. The train is the 05.15 Penzance–London Paddington.

Colin J. Marsden

Class 47 No. 47345 passes the M27 motorway near Eastleigh with the daily 09.00 Southampton–Coatbridge service on 26th April 1996. This loco carries Freightliner livery.
Nic Joynson

Still carrying the obsolete Trainload Metals livery, Class 56 No. 56061 passes Clay Cross with a Tees yard to Etruria service on 31st May 1996.

Hugh Ballantyne

Names:

31102 Cricklewood
31105 Bescot TMD
31106 The Blackcountryman
31130 Calder Hall Power Station
31146 Brush Veteran
31147 Floreat Salopia
31233 Severn Valley Railway

CLASS 31/4. Equipped with Train Heating. RA6.
CLASS 31/5. Train Heating Equipment isolated. RA6.

31405	**M**	LBDB	BS	Mappa Mundi
31407	**ML**	ENTN	TO	
31408		LCXX	SP (S)	
31410	**RR**	LWNW	SP	
31411	**D**	LCXX	BS (U)	
31512	**C**	LWNW	SP	
31413	**0**	LCXX	BS (U)	
31514	**C**	LWNW	SP	
31415		LCXX	BS (U)	
31516	**C**	LCXX	BS (U)	
31417	**D**	LCXX	BS (U)	
31519	**C**	LCXX	SP (U)	
31420	**M**	LBDB	BS	
31421	**RR**	LWNW	SP	
31422	**M**	LBDB	BS	
31423	**M**	LCWX	BS (U)	Jerome K. Jerome
31524	**C**	LCWX	BS (U)	
31526	**C**	LCXX	BS (U)	
31427		LCWX	SP (S)	
31530	**C**	LCWX	BS (U)	
31531	**C**	ENXX	TO (U)	
31432		LCWX	SP (U)	
31533	**C**	LCXX	BS (U)	
31434		LWNW	SP	
31435	**C**	LCWX	BS (U)	
31537	**C**	LCWX	BS (U)	
31538	**C**	LCWX	SP (S)	
31439	**RR**	LWNW	SP	North Yorkshire Moors Railway
31541	**C**	ENXX	TO (U)	
31444	**C**	LCXX	SP (U)	
31545		LBDB	BS	
31546	**C**	LCWX	BS (U)	
31548	**C**	LCXX	BS (U)	
31549	**C**	ENXX	TO (U)	
31450		LWNW	SP	
31551	**C**	ENXX	TO (U)	
31552	**C**	ENXX	TO (S)	
31554	**C**	LBDB	BS	
31455	**RR**	LCWX	SP (U)	

31556	C	LCWX	SP (U)
31558	C	ENXX	TO (U)
31459		ENXX	TO (U)
31461	D	ENXX	TO (U)
31462	D	LBDB	BS
31563	C	ENXX	TO (U)
31465	RR	LWNW	SP
31466	C	ENTN	TO
31467		LWNW	SP
31468	C	LBDB	BS	The Enginemen's Fund

CLASS 33   BRCW TYPE 3   Bo – Bo

Built: 1960 – 62 by the Birmingham Railway Carriage & Wagon Company, Smethwick.
Engine: Sulzer 8LDA28 of 1160 kW (1550 hp) at 750 rpm.
Main Generator: Crompton Parkinson CG391B1.
Traction Motors: Crompton Parkinson C171C2.
Max. Tractive Effort: 200 kN (45000 lbf).
Cont. Tractive Effort: 116 kN (26000 lbf) at 17.5 m.p.h.
Power At Rail: 906 kW (1215 hp).   **Length over Buffers:** 15.47 m.
Brake Force: 35 t.   **Wheel Diameter:** 1092 mm.
Design Speed: 85 m.p.h.   **Weight:** 77.5 t (78.5 t Class 33/1).
Max. Speed: 60 m.p.h.   **RA:** 6.
Train Heating: Electric (y isolated). **ETH Index:** 48.
Train Brakes: Air & vacuum.
Multiple Working: Blue Star Coupling Code.
Communication Equipment: Cab to shore radio-telephone.

Formerly numbered in series 6500 – 97 but not in order. 33116 carries its original number D 6535.

Class 33/0. Standard Design.

33002	y	C	ENXX	SL (U)	
33008	y	G	ENXX	SL (U)	Eastleigh
33012	e		ENXX	SL (S)	
33019	e	C	EWDB	SL	Griffon
33023	e		ENXX	SL (U)	
33025	e	C	EWDB	SL	Sultan
33026	e	C	EWDB	SL	Seafire
33029	e		ENXX	SL (U)	
33030	e	C	EWDB	SL	
33046	y	C	EWDB	SL	Merlin
33048	es		ENXX	SL (S)	
33051	e	C	EWDB	SL	Shakespeare Cliff
33052	e		ENXX	SL (S)	
33053	e	FA	ENXX	SL (U)	
33057	ys	C	ENXX	SL (U)	Seagull
33063	ys	FM	ENXX	SL (S)	
33065	e	C	ENXX	SL (S)	

Class 33/1. Fitted with Buckeye Couplings & SR Multiple Working Equipment for use with SR EMUs, TC stock & class 73.

Also fitted with flashing light adaptor for use on Weymouth Quay line.

33103	e	**C**	ENXX	SL (S)
33109	e	**D**	EWDB	SL
33116	e		EWDB	SL	Hertfordshire Rail Tours
33117	e		ENXX	SL (U)

Class 33/2. Built to Former Loading Gauge of Tonbridge – Battle Line.

33202	ys	**C**	EWDB	SL	The Burma Star
33204	es	**FM**	ENXX	SL (U)
33205	es	**FD**	ENZX	SL (U)
33207	ys	**FA**	ENXX	SL (U)
33208	es	**C**	EWDB	SL

CLASS 37   ENGLISH ELECTRIC TYPE 3   Co–Co

Built: 1960 – 5 by English Electric Company at Vulcan Foundry, Newton le Willows or Robert Stephenson & Hawthorn, Darlington. 37003 – 115/340/1/3/ 350/1/9 with the exception of 37019*/047/065*/072*/073/074/075*/ 100* (* one end only) retain box-type route indicators, the remainder having central headcode panels/marker lamps.
Engine: English Electric 12CSVT of 1300 kW (1750 hp) at 850 rpm.
Main Generator: English Electric 822/10G.
Traction Motors: English Electric 538/A.
Max. Tractive Effort: 245 kN (55500 lbf).
Cont. Tractive Effort: 156 kN (35000 lbf) at 13.6 m.p.h.
Power At Rail: 932 kW (1250 hp).   **Length over Buffers:** 18.75 m.
Brake Force: 50 t.   **Wheel Diameter:** 1092 mm.
Design Speed: 90 m.p.h.   **Weight:** 103 – 108 t.
Max. Speed: 80 m.p.h.   **RA:** 5 or 7.
Train Heating: Electric (Class 37/4 only). **ETH Index:** 30.
Train Brakes: Air & Vacuum.
Multiple Working: Blue Star Coupling Code.
Communication Equipment: Cab to shore radio-telephone.

Non-standard livery: 37116 is BR blue with Transrail markings.

a Vacuum brake isolated.

Formerly numbered 6600 – 8, 6700 – 6999 (not in order).
37274 is the second loco to carry that number. It was renumbered to avoid confusion with Class 37/3 locos.

Class 37/0. Unrefurbished Locos. Technical details as above. RA5.

37003	+	**C**	FDYX	IM (U)
37010		**C**	ENTN	TO
37012		**C**	ENTN	TO
37013	+	**ML**	ENTN	TO
37019	+	**FD**	FDYX	IM (U)
37023		**ML**	EWDB	SF	Stratford TMD Quality Approved

37025	**BR**	LBLB	BS	Inverness TMD Quality Assured
37026 +	**FD**	LCWX	SP (S)	
37035	**C**	ENXX	SL (U)	
37037	**FM**	EWDB	SL	
37038	**C**	ENTN	TO	
37040	**EW**	EWRB	SL	
37042 +	**EW**	ENTN	TO	
37043	**CT**	LGBM	ML	
37045 +	**F**	FDYX	TE (U)	
37046	**C**	ENTN	TO	
37047 +	**ML**	EWDB	SF	
37048	**FM**	ENXX	TO (U)	
37051	**EW**	ENTN	TO	Merehead
37054	**C**	EWDB	SL	
37055 +	**ML**	ENTN	TO	RAIL Celebrity
37057 +	**EW**	ENTN	TO	Viking
37058 +	**C**	FDYX	IM (U)	
37059 +	**FD**	FDYX	IM (U)	
37063 +	**FD**	FDYX	TE (U)	
37065 +	**ML**	ENTN	TO	
37066 +	**C**	LCWX	SP (U)	
37068 +	**FD**	FDYX	IM (U)	
37069 +	**C**	LGBM	ML	
37071 +	**C**	LBLB	BS	
37072 +	**D**	ENTN	TO	
37073 +	**FT**	LBLB	BS	Fort William/An Gearasdan
37074 +	**ML**	EWDB	SL	
37075 +	**F**	FDYX	TE (U)	
37077	**ML**	EWDB	SL	
37078 +	**FS**	LCXX	ML (U)	
37079 +	**FD**	ENTN	TO	
37083 +	**C**	FDYX	IM (U)	
37087	**C**	LBLB	BS	
37088	**CT**	LCWX	ML (U)	Clydesdale
37092	**C**	ENXX	TO (U)	
37095 +	**C**	LBLB	BS	
37097	**C**	ENTN	TO	
37098 +	**C**	ENTN	TO	
37099	**C**	LCWX	BS (U)	
37100 +	**FT**	LGBM	ML	
37101 +	**FD**	FDYX	IM (U)	
37104	**C**	FDYX	IM (U)	
37106 +	**C**	EWDB	SF	
37107 +	**FD**	LCWX	SP (U)	
37108 +	**F**	LCWX	BS (U)	
37109	**EW**	EWDB	SL	
37110 +	**F**	FDYX	IM (U)	
37111	**FT**	LCWX	BS (U)	
37114 +	**EW**	ENTN	TO	City of Worcester
37116 +	**0**	LBLB	BS	Sister Dora
37131 +	**F**	FDRI	IM	

37133	**C**	LBSB	BS	
37137	**FM**	ENTN	TO	
37139 +	**FC**	FDYX	IM (U)	
37140	**C**	EWDB	SF	
37141	**C**	LBLB	BS	
37142	**C**	LBLB	BS	
37144 r	**FA**	FDYX	IM (U)	
37146	**C**	LBLB	BS	
37152	**I**	LGBM	ML	
37153	**CT**	LGBM	ML	
37154 +	**FT**	LBSB	BS	
37156 r	**FT**	LCWX	ML (S)	
37158	**C**	LBLB	BS	
37162 +	**D**	ENTN	TO	
37165 +	**C**	LGBM	ML	
37167 +	**ML**	EWDB	SL	
37170 r	**C**	LGBM	ML	
37174	**C**	EWRB	SL	
37175	**C**	LGBM	ML	
37178 +	**F**	LBSB	BS	
37184	**C**	LCWX	BS (U)	
37185 +	**C**	ENTN	TO	Lea & Perrins
37188	**C**	LCWX	BS (U)	
37191	**C**	LBSB	BS	
37194 +	**FM**	EWRB	SL	British International Freight Association
37196	**C**	LBSB	BS	
37197 +	**CT**	LNSK	CF	
37198 +	**ML**	EWDB	SL	
37201	**CT**	LCWX	BS (S) Saint Margaret	
37203	**ML**	EWDB	SL	
37207	**C**	LCWX	BS (U)	
37209	**BR**	FDYX	IM (U)	
37211	**C**	LBLB	BS	
37212 +	**FT**	LBLB	BS	
37213 +	**FC**	LCWX	CF (U)	
37214 +	**FA**	LBLB	BS	
37216 r+	**ML**	EWDB	SF	Great Eastern
37217 +		FDYX	IM (U)	
37218 +	**F**	FDYX	IM (U)	
37219 r	**ML**	EWDB	SL	
37220 +	**EW**	EWRB	SL	
37221	**FT**	LGBM	ML	
37222 +	**FM**	ENTN	TO	
37223 +	**FC**	FDYX	IM (U)	
37225 +	**F**	FDRI	IM	
37227 +	**FM**	ENTN	TO	
37229 +	**FC**	LNSK	CF	
37230 +	**CT**	LNSK	CF	
37232 r	**CT**	LCWX	ML (U) The Institution of Railway Signal Engineers	
37235 +	**F**	FDYX	IM (U)	

37238	+	F	ENTN	TO		
37240	+	C	LBLB	BS		
37241		F	ENXX	SF	(U)	
37242	+	ML	EWDB	SF		
37244	+	F	ENTN	TO		
37245		C	EWRB	SL		
37248	+	ML	ENTN	TO		Midland Railway Centre
37250	+	FT	LGBM	ML		
37251	+	I	LCWX	ML	(U)	The Northern Lights
37254	+	C	LNSK	CF		
37255	+	C	LBSB	BS		
37258	+	C	LBSB	BS		
37261	+	FD	LGBM	ML		Caithness
37262	+	D	LBSB	BS		Dounreay
37263		C	LNSK	CF		
37264		C	ENTN	TO		
37274	+	ML	EWDB	SL		
37275	+		LNSK	CF		Oor Wullie
37278	+	FC	ENXX	TO	(U)	
37293	+	ML	EWRB	SL		
37294	+	C	LGBM	ML		
37298	+	F	FDYX	IM	(U)	

Class 37/3. Unrefurbished locos fitted with regeared (CP7) bogies.
Details as Class 37/0 except:
Max. Tractive Effort: 250 kN (56180 lbf).
Cont. Tractive Effort: 184 kN (41250 lbf) at 11.4 m.p.h.

37330	+	EW	LBSB	BS		
37331		F	FDYX	IM	(U)	
37332	+	FC	FDRI	IM		The Coal Merchants' Association
						of Scotland
37333	+	FD	FDYX	IM	(U)	
37334	+	F	LBSB	BS		
37335	+	F	FDYX	IM	(U)	
37340	+	FD	FDYX	IM	(U)	
37341	+	F	FDYX	TE	(U)	
37343		C	FDYX	IM	(U)	
37344	+	FD	FDYX	IM	(U)	
37350	+	FP	FDRI	IM		
37351	+	CT	LGBM	ML		
37358		F	FDRI	IM		
37359		FP	FDYX	TE	(U)	
37370		EW	EWRB	SL		
37371	+	ML	EWDB	SL		
37372		ML	EWRB	SL		
37375	+	ML	EWDB	SL		
37376	+	FC	ENTN	TO		
37377	+	C	EWDB	SL		
37379		ML	EWDB	SF		Ipswich WRD Quality Assured
37380		FM	EWRB	SL		
37381	+	FD	FDYX	IM	(U)	

37382   **FP** FDYX   IM (U)

Class 37/4. Refurbished locos fitted with train heating. Main generator replaced by alternator. Regeared (CP7) bogies. Details as class 37/0 except:

Main Alternator: Brush BA1005A.
Max. Tractive Effort: 256 kN (57440 lbf).
Cont. Tractive Effort: 184 kN (41250 lbf) at 11.4 m.p.h.
Power At Rail: 935 kW (1254 hp).
All have twin fuel tanks.

37401 r	**FT**	LGHM	ML	Mary Queen of Scots
37402 r	**F**	LWMC	CD	Bont Y Bermo
37403 r	**G**	LGHM	ML	Ben Cruachan
37404 r	**FT**	LGHM	ML	Loch Long
37405 r	**M**	LWCW	SP	Strathclyde Region
37406 r	**EW**	LGHM	ML	The Saltaire Society
37407 r	**FT**	LWCW	SP	Blackpool Tower
37408	**BR**	LWMC	CD	Loch Rannoch
37409 r	**FT**	LGHM	ML	Loch Awe
37410 r	**FT**	LGHM	ML	Aluminium 100
37411	**FT**	LNCK	CF	
37412	**FT**	LNCK	CF	Driver John Elliot
37413 r	**FT**	LWCW	SP	Loch Eil Outward Bound
37414 r	**RR**	LWMC	CD	Cathays C&W Works 1846 – 1993
37415 r	**EW**	LWCW	SP	
37416 r	**EW**	LNCK	CF	
37417 r	**F**	LWMC	CD	Highland Region
37418 r	**EW**	LWMC	CD	East Lancashire Railway
37419 r	**EW**	LWCW	SP	
37420 r	**RR**	LWMC	CD	The Scottish Hosteller
37421 r	**RR**	LWMC	CD	The Kingsman
37422 r	**RR**	LWMC	CD	Robert F. Fairlie Locomotive Engineer 1831 – 1885
37423 r	**FT**	LCWX	ML(U)	Sir Murray Morrison 1873 – 1948 Pioneer of British Aluminium Industry
37424 r	**FT**	LGHM	ML	
37425 r	**RR**	LWMC	CD	Sir Robert McAlpine/ Concrete Bob (opp. sides)
37426 r	**M**	LWCW	SP	
37427 r	**EW**	LCWX	CD	Highland Enterprise
37428 r	**FT**	LGHM	ML	David Lloyd George
37429 r	**RR**	LWMC	CD	Eisteddfod Genedlaethol
37430 r	**FT**	LGHM	ML	Cwmbrân
37431 r	**M**	LCWX	ML (U)	

Class 37/5. Refurbished locos. Main generator replaced by alternator. Regeared (CP7) bogies. Details as class 37/4 except:

Max. Tractive Effort: 248 kN (55590 lbf).
All have twin fuel tanks.

37503	**EW**	FDRI	IM	
37505	**FT**	LBLB	BS	British Steel Workington
37509	**FT**	LWCW	SP	
37510	**I**	LGBM	ML	
37513	**LH**	FDCI	IM	
37515 s	**LH**	FDCI	IM	
37516 s	**LH**	FDCI	IM	
37517 ars	**EW**	FDCI	IM	
37518	**FS**	LWCW	SP	
37519	**FS**	FDCI	IM	
37520	**FS**	LWCW	SP	
37521	**FP**	LNLK	CF	

Class 37/6. Refurbished locos for use on Channel Tunnel Night services. All have train air brakes only, UIC brake and coaching stock jumpers, RCH jumpers, ETH through wires.

37601 (37501)	**E**	GPSV	OC
37602 (37502)	**E**	GPSV	OC
37603 (37504)	**E**	GPSV	OC
37604 (37506)	**E**	GPSV	OC
37605 (37507)	**E**	GPSV	OC
37606 (37508)	**E**	GPSV	OC
37607 (37511)	**E**	GPSV	OC
37608 (37512)	**E**	GPSV	OC
37609 (37514)	**E**	GPSV	OC
37610 (37687)	**E**	GPSV	OC
37611 (37690)	**E**	GPSV	OC
37612 (37691)	**E**	GPSV	OC

Class 37/5 continued.

37667 s	**F**	EWDB	SF	
37668 s	**EW**	LNLK	CF	
37669	**FT**	LNLK	CF	
37670	**FT**	LNLK	CF	St. Blazey T&RS Depot
37671	**FT**	LNLK	CF	Tre Pol and Pen
37672 s	**FD**	LNLK	CF	Freight Transport Association
37673	**FT**	LNLK	CF	
37674	**FT**	LNLK	CF	Saint Blaise Church 1445 – 1995
37675 s	**FT**	LGBM	ML	
37676	**F**	EWDB	SF	
37677	**F**	FDCI	IM	
37678	**FA**	EWDB	SF	
37679	**F**	EWDB	SF	
37680	**FA**	FDCI	IM	
37682 r	**EW**	FDCI	IM	Hartlepool Pipe Mill
37683	**FT**	LGBM	ML	

37684	**EW** FDCI	IM	Peak National Park
37685	**I** LGBM	ML	
37686	**FA** FDCI	IM	
37688	**EW** FDCI	IM	Great Rocks
37689 s	**F** FDCI	IM	
37692 s	**FC** LGBM	ML	The Lass O' Ballochmyle
37693 s	**FT** LGBM	ML	
37694 s	**FC** FDCI	IM	
37695 s	**FT** LBLB	BS	
37696 s	**FT** LNLK	CF	
37697 s	**EW** FDCI	IM	
37698 s	**LH** FDCI	IM	
37699	**FC** FDYX	IM (U)	

Class 37/7. Refurbished locos. Main generator replaced by alternator. Regeared (CP7) bogies. Ballast weights added. Details as class 37/4 except:

Main Alternator: GEC G564AZ (37796 – 803) Brush BA1005A (others).
Max. Tractive Effort: 276 kN (62000 lbf).
Weight: 120 t.   **RA:** 7.
All have twin fuel tanks.

37701 s	**FT** LNCK	CF	
37702 s	**FT** LGBM	ML	Taff Merthyr
37703 s	**FM** EWDB	SL	
37704 s	**EW** LNCK	CF	
37705	**FM** EWDB	SL	
37706	**EW** FDCI	IM	
37707	**EW** FDCI	IM	
37708	**FP** FDCI	IM	
37709	**FM** EWDB	SL	
37710	**LH** FDCI	IM	
37711	**FS** FDCI	IM	
37712	**FP** LGBM	ML	Teesside Steelmaster
37713	**LH** FDCI	IM	
37714	**FS** LGBM	ML	
37715	**FM** ENTN	TO	British Petroleum
37716	**FS** FDCI	IM	British Steel Corby
37717	**EW** FDCI	IM	Maltby Lilly Hall Junior School Rotherham Railsafe Trophy Winners 1996
37718	**EW** FDCI	IM	
37719	**FP** FDCI	IM	
37796 s	**FC** LGBM	ML	
37797 s	**FC** LGBM	ML	
37798 s	**ML** ENTN	TO	
37799 s	**FT** LGBM	ML	Sir Dyfed/County of Dyfed
37800 s	**FM** EWDB	SL	
37801 s	**EW** LGBM	ML	
37802 s	**FT** LGBM	ML	
37803 s	**ML** EWDB	SL	
37883	**EW** FDCI	IM	
37884	**LH** FDCI	IM	Gartcosh

37885	U	FDCI	IM
37886	EW	FDCI	IM
37887 s	FT	LNCK	CF
37888	F	FDCI	IM
37889	FT	LNCK	CF
37890 a	FM	EWDB	SL
37891	FM	EWDB	SL
37892	FM	EWDB	SL
37893	EW	LGBM	ML
37894 s	FC	LNCK	CF
37895 s	EW	LNCK	CF
37896 s	FT	LNCK	CF
37897 s	FT	LNCK	CF
37898 s	FT	LNCK	CF
37899 s	FC	LNCK	CF

37887: Caerphilly Castle/Castell Caerffili
37890: The Railway Observer
37892: Ripple Lane
37898: Cwmbargoed DP
37899: County of West Glamorgan/ Sir Gorllewin Morgannwg

Class 37/9. Refurbished Locos. Fitted with manufacturers prototype power units and ballast weights. Main generator replaced by alternator. Details as Class 37/0 except:

Engine: Mirrlees MB275T of 1340 kW (1800 hp) at 1000 rpm (37901 – 4), Ruston RK270T of 1340 kW (1800 hp) at 900 rpm (37905 – 6).
Main Alternator: Brush BA1005A (GEC G564, 37905/6).
Max. Tractive Effort: 279 kN (62680 lbf).
Cont. Tractive Effort: 184 kN (41250 lbf) at 11.4 m.p.h.
Weight: 120 t.   **RA:** 7.
All have twin fuel tanks.

37901	FT	LNCK	CF
37902	FS	LNCK	CF
37903	FS	LNCK	CF
37904	FS	LCWX	CF (U)
37905 s	FS	LNCK	CF
37906 s	FT	LNCK	CF

37901: Mirrlees Pioneer
37905: Vulcan Enterprise

CLASS 43   HST POWER CAR   Bo – Bo

Built: 1976 – 82 by BREL Crewe Works. Formerly numbered as coaching stock but now classified as locomotives. Fitted with luggage compartment.
Engine: Paxman Valenta 12RP200L (Paxman VP185*) of 1680 kW (2250 hp) at 1500 rpm.
Main Alternator: Brush BA1001B.
Traction Motors: Brush TMH68 – 46 or GEC G417AZ (43124 – 151/180). Frame mounted.
Max. Tractive Effort: 80 kN (17980 lbf).
Cont. Tractive Effort: 46 kN (10340 lbf) at 64.5 m.p.h.
Power At Rail: 1320 kW (1770 hp).   **ETH:** Non standard 3-phase system.
Brake Force: 35 t.   **Length over Buffers:** 17.79 m.
Weight: 70 t.   **Wheel Diameter:** 1020 mm.
Max. Speed: 125 m.p.h.   **RA:** 5.

Train Brakes: Air.
Multiple Working: With one other similar vehicle.
Communication Equipment: All equipped with driver – guard telephone and cab to shore radio-telephone.

§ Modified to be able to remotely control a class 91 locomotive and to be remotely controlled by a class 91 locomotive. Fitted with buffers. Tdm and Class 91 control equipment now isolated.

Note: Cross Country Trains and Midland Main Line locos are owned by Porterbrook Leasing Company. Great North Eastern Railway and Great Western Trains locos are owned by Angel Train Contracts. The above does not apply to Cross Country Trains locos 43006 – 8, 43178/184 which are owned by Angel Train Contracts and Porterbrook leasing-owned 43104 and 43180 are spare power cars which are used to cover for failures and shortages.

43002	I	IWRP	PM	
43003	I	IWRP	PM	
43004	I	IWRP	PM	
43005	I	IWRP	PM	
43006	I	ICCP	LA	
43007	I	ICCP	LA	
43008	I	ICCP	LA	
43009	I	IWRP	PM	
43010	I	IWRP	PM	
43011	I	IWRP	PM	Reader 125
43012	I	IWRP	PM	
43013 §	I	ICCS	EC	CROSSCOUNTRY VOYAGER
43014 §	I	ICCS	EC	
43015	**GW**	IWRP	PM	
43016	I	IWRP	PM	
43017	I	IWRP	LA	
43018	I	IWRP	LA	
43019	I	IWRP	LA	City of Swansea/Dinas Abertawe
43020	I	IWRP	LA	John Grooms
43021	I	IWRP	LA	
43022	I	IWRP	LA	
43023	I	IWRP	LA	County of Cornwall
43024	I	IWRP	LA	
43025	I	IWRP	LA	Exeter
43026	I	IWRP	LA	City of Westminster
43027	I	IWRP	LA	Glorious Devon
43028	I	IWCP	LO	
43029	I	IWCP	LO	
43030	I	IWRP	PM	
43031	I	IWRP	PM	
43032	I	IWRP	PM	The Royal Regiment of Wales
43033	I	IWRP	PM	
43034	I	IWRP	PM	The Black Horse
43035	I	IWRP	PM	
43036	I	IWRP	PM	
43037	I	IWRP	PM	

43038	I	IECP	NL	National Railway Museum
				The First Ten Years 1975 – 1985
43039	I	IECP	NL	
43040	I	IWRP	PM	
43041	I	IWCP	LO	City of Discovery
43042	I	IWCP	LO	
43043	I	IMLP	NL	
43044	I	IMLP	NL	Borough of Kettering
43045	I	IMLP	NL	The Grammar School Doncaster AD 1350
43046	I	IMLP	NL	Royal Philharmonic
43047 *	I	IMLP	NL	Rotherham Enterprise
43048	I	IMLP	NL	
43049	I	IMLP	NL	Neville Hill
43050	I	IMLP	NL	
43051	I	IMLP	NL	The Duke and Duchess of York
43052	I	IMLP	NL	City of Peterborough
43053	I	IMLP	NL	Leeds United
43054	I	IMLP	NL	
43055	I	IMLP	NL	Sheffield Star
43056	I	IMLP	NL	University of Bradford
43057	I	IMLP	NL	Bounds Green
43058	I	IMLP	NL	
43059 *	I	IMLP	NL	
43060	I	IMLP	NL	County of Leicestershire
43061	I	IMLP	NL	City of Lincoln
43062	I	ICCS	EC	
43063	I	ICCS	EC	
43064	I	IMLP	NL	City of York
43065 §	I	ICCS	EC	City of Edinburgh
43066	I	IMLP	NL	Nottingham Playhouse
43067 §	I	ICCS	EC	
43068 §	I	ICCS	EC	
43069	I	ICCS	EC	
43070	I	ICCS	EC	
43071	I	ICCS	EC	Forward Birmingham
43072	I	IMLP	NL	Derby Etches Park
43073	I	IMLP	NL	
43074 *	I	IMLP	NL	
43075 *	I	IMLP	NL	
43076	I	IMLP	NL	BBC East Midlands Today
43077	I	IMLP	NL	County of Nottingham
43078	I	ICCS	EC	Golowan Festival Penzance
43079	I	ICCS	EC	
43080 §	I	ICCS	EC	
43081	I	IMLP	NL	
43082	I	IMLP	NL	
43083	I	IMLP	NL	
43084 §	I	ICCS	EC	County of Derbyshire
43085	I	IMLP	NL	City of Bradford
43086	I	ICCS	EC	
43087	I	ICCS	EC	

43088	I	ICCS	EC	XIII Commonwealth Games Scotland 1986
43089	I	ICCS	EC	
43090	I	ICCS	EC	
43091	I	ICCP	LA	Edinburgh Military Tattoo
43092	I	ICCS	EC	
43093	I	ICCS	EC	York Festival '88
43094	I	ICCS	EC	
43095	I	IECP	NL	
43096	I	IECP	NL	The Queens Own Hussars
43097	I	ICCS	EC	
43098	I	ICCS	EC	
43099	I	ICCS	EC	
43100	I	ICCS	EC	Craigentinny
43101	I	ICCP	LA	Edinburgh International Festival
43102	I	ICCP	LA	
43103	I	ICCP	LA	John Wesley
43104	I	IECP	EC	County of Cleveland
43105	I	IECP	NL	Hartlepool
43106	I	IECP	NL	Songs of Praise
43107	I	IECP	NL	
43108	I	IECP	NL	
43109	I	IECP	NL	Yorkshire Evening Press
43110	I	IECP	EC	Darlington
43111	I	IECP	EC	
43112	I	IECP	EC	
43113	I	IECP	EC	City of Newcastle-upon-Tyne
43114	I	IECP	EC	National Garden Festival Gateshead 1990
43115	I	IECP	EC	Yorkshire Cricket Academy
43116	I	IECP	EC	City of Kingston Upon Hull
43117	GN	IECP	EC	
43118	GN	IECP	EC	Charles Wesley
43119	I	IECP	EC	
43120	GN	IECP	EC	
43121	I	ICCP	LA	West Yorkshire Metropolitan County
43122	I	ICCP	LA	South Yorkshire Metropolitan County
43123 §	I	ICCS	EC	
43124	I	IWRP	PM	
43125	I	IWRP	PM	Merchant Venturer
43126	I	IWRP	PM	City of Bristol
43127	I	IWRP	PM	
43128	I	IWRP	PM	University of Swansea
43129	GW	IWRP	PM	
43130	I	IWRP	PM	Sulis Minerva
43131	I	IWRP	PM	Sir Felix Pole
43132	I	IWRP	PM	
43133	I	IWRP	PM	
43134	I	IWRP	PM	County of Somerset
43135	GW	IWRP	PM	
43136	I	IWRP	PM	
43137	I	IWRP	PM	
43138	I	IWRP	PM	

43139	**GW**	IWRP	PM	
43140	I	IWRP	PM	
43141	I	IWRP	PM	
43142	I	IWRP	PM	
43143	I	IWRP	PM	
43144	I	IWRP	PM	
43145	I	IWRP	PM	
43146	I	IWRP	PM	
43147	I	IWRP	PM	The Red Cross
43148	I	IWRP	PM	
43149	I	IWRP	PM	BBC Wales Today
43150	I	IWRP	PM	Bristol Evening Post
43151	I	IWRP	PM	
43152	I	IWRP	PM	
43153	I	ICCP	LA	University of Durham
43154	I	ICCP	LA	INTERCITY
43155	I	ICCP	LA	BBC Look North
43156	I	ICCP	LA	
43157	I	ICCP	LA	Yorkshire Evening Post
43158	I	ICCP	LA	Dartmoor The Pony Express
43159	I	ICCP	LA	
43160	I	ICCP	LA	Storm Force
43161	I	ICCP	LA	Reading Evening Post
43162	I	ICCP	LA	Borough of Stevenage
43163	I	IWRP	LA	
43164	I	IWCP	LO	
43165	I	IWCP	LO	
43166	I	IWCP	LO	
43167 *	I	IECP	NL	
43168 *	**GW**	IWRP	LA	
43169 *	I	IWRP	LA	The National Trust
43170 *	I	IWRP	LA	Edward Paxman
43171	I	IWRP	LA	
43172	I	IWRP	LA	
43173	I	IWRP	LA	Swansea University
43174	I	IWRP	LA	
43175	I	IWRP	LA	
43176	I	IWRP	LA	
43177	I	IWRP	LA	University of Exeter
43178	I	ICCP	LA	
43179	I	IWRP	LA	Pride of Laira
43180	I	IMLP	NL	
43181	I	IWRP	LA	Devonport Royal Dockyard 1693-1993
43182	I	IWRP	LA	
43183	**GW**	IWRP	LA	
43184	I	ICCP	LA	
43185	**GW**	IWRP	LA	Great Western
43186	I	IWRP	LA	Sir Francis Drake
43187	I	IWRP	LA	
43188	I	IWRP	LA	City of Plymouth
43189	I	IWRP	LA	RAILWAY HERITAGE TRUST

43190	I	IWRP	LA	
43191	GW	IWRP	LA	Seahawk
43192	I	IWRP	LA	City of Truro
43193	I	ICCP	LA	Plymouth SPIRIT OF DISCOVERY
43194	I	ICCP	LA	
43195	I	ICCP	LA	British Red Cross 125th Birthday 1995
43196	I	ICCP	LA	The Newspaper Society Founded 1836
43197	I	ICCP	LA	Railway Magazine 1897 Centenary 1997
43198	I	ICCP	LA	

CLASS 46   BR TYPE 4   1Co – Co1

Built: 1962 by BR Derby Locomotive Works.
Engine: Sulzer 12LDA28B of 1860 kW (2500 hp) at 750 rpm.
Main Generator: Brush TG160-60.
Traction Motors: Brush TM73-68 Mk3 (axle hung).
Max. Tractive Effort: 245 kN (55000 lbf).
Cont. Tractive Effort: 141 kN (31600 lbf) at 22.3 m.p.h.
Power At Rail: 1460 kW (1960 hp).   **Length over Buffers:** 20.70 m.
Brake Force: 63 t.   **Wheel Diameter:** 914/1143 mm.
Design Speed: 90 m.p.h.   **Weight:** 141 t.
Max. Speed: 75 m.p.h.   **RA:** 7.
Train Brakes: Air & vacuum.
Multiple Working: Not equipped.

Owned by Carriage & Traction Company Ltd.

Carries original number D 172.

46035	G		CQ	Ixion

CLASS 47   BRUSH TYPE 4   Co – Co

Built: 1963 – 67 by Brush Traction, Loughborough or BR Crewe Works.
Engine: Sulzer 12LDA28C of 1920 kW (2580 hp) at 750 rpm.
Main Generator: Brush TG160-60 Mk2, TG160-60 Mk4 or TM172-50 Mk1.
Traction Motors: Brush TM64-68 Mk1 or Mk1A (axle hung).
Max. Tractive Effort: 267 kN (60000 lbf).
Cont. Tractive Effort: 133 kN (30000 lbf) at 26 m.p.h.
Power At Rail: 1550 kW (2080 hp).   **Length over Buffers:** 19.38 m.
Brake Force: 61 t.   **Wheel Diameter:** 1143 mm.
Design Speed: 95 m.p.h.   **Weight:** 120.5 – 125 t.
Max. Speed: various.   **RA:** 6 or 7.
Train Brakes: Air & vacuum.
Multiple Working: Green Circle (m) or Blue Star (*) Coupling Code. Otherwise not equipped.
ETH Index (47/4, 47/6 and 47/7): 66 (75 Class 47/6).
Communication Equipment: Cab to shore radio-telephone.

Non standard liveries:

47145 is dark blue with Railfreight Distribution markings.
47798/9 are Royal train purple.
47803 is grey, red and yellow.

Formerly numbered 1100 – 11, 1500 – 1999 not in order.

47052/60/142/7/57/87/97/206/12/25/31/70/9/83/9/96,
47301/5/17/22.37/9/45/7/9/54/8/71/6/7 are owned by Porterbrook Leasing
Company. Other Freightliner locos are owned by Freightliner 1995 Ltd.
All PWLO and PWLS locos are owned by Carriage & Traction Co. Ltd.
Cross Country Trains and Great Western Trains locos are owned by Porterbrook
Leasing Company.

a Vacuum brake isolated.

Class 47/0. Built with train heating boiler. RA6. Max. Speed 75 m.p.h.

47004	**G**	ENRN	TO	Old Oak Common
				Traction & Rolling Stock Depot
47016	**FO**	ENRN	TO	ATLAS
47019	**FO**	DHLT	CD (U)	
47033 am +	**FE**	DAET	TI	The Royal Logistics Corps
47049 am +	**FE**	DAET	TI	GEFCO
47051 am +	**FE**	DAET	TI	
47052	**FF**	DFLT	CD	
47053 am +	**FE**	DAET	TI	Dollands Moor International
47060 a	**F**	DFLT	CD	
47079	**FE**	DHLT	CD (U)	
47085 am +	**FE**	DAET	TI	REPTA 1893 – 1993
47095 am +	**FE**	DAET	TI	
47114 am +	**FD**	DFLM	CD	
47125 am +	**FE**	DAET	TI	
47142	**FR**	DHLT	CD	
47144 am +	**FD**	DAXT	TI	
47145 am	**O**	DAET	TI	
47146 am	**FE**	DAET	TI	Loughborough Grammar School
47147	**F**	DFLT	CD	
47150 am +	**FE**	DAET	TI	
47152 am +	**FF**	DFLM	CD	
47156 am +	**FD**	DHLT	CD	
47157	**FF**	DFLT	CD	Johnson Stevens Agencies
47186 am +	**FE**	DAET	TI	Catcliffe Demon
47187	**F**	DHLT	CD	
47188 am +	**FE**	DAET	TI	
47193	**FP**	LCWX	BS (U)	
47194 am +	**FD**	DAET	TI	
47197	**F**	DFLT	CD	
47200 am +	**FE**	DAET	TI	Herbert Austin
47201 am +	**FE**	DAET	TI	
47204 am +	**F**	DFLM	CD	
47205 am +	**FF**	DFLM	CD	
47206	**FF**	DFLT	CD	The Morris Dancer
47207	**F**	DHLT	CD	
47209 am +	**FF**	DFLM	CD	
47210 am +	**FD**	DAET	TI	
47211 am +	**FD**	DAET	TI	
47212 +	**F**	DFLT	CD	

47213	am +	**FD**	DAET	TI	Marchwood Military Port
47217	am +	**FE**	DAET	TI	
47218	am +	**FE**	DAET	TI	United Transport Europe
47219	am +	**FE**	DAET	TI	Arnold Kunzler
47221	+	**FP**	FDYX	IM (U)	
47222	am +	**FD**	DAYX	TI (U)	
47223	+	**F**	ENXX	SF (U)	
47224	+	**FP**	FDKI	IM	
47225		**FF**	DFLT	CD	
47226	am +	**FD**	DAET	TI	
47228	am +	**FE**	DAET	TI	axial
47229	am +	**FE**	DAET	TI	
47231		**F**	DFLT	CD	
47234	am +	**FE**	DFLM	CD	
47236	am +	**FE**	DAXT	TI	ROVER GROUP QUALITY ASSURED
47237	am +	**FE**	DAET	TI	
47238		**FD**	LCXX	BS (U)	Bescot Yard
47241	am +	**FE**	DAET	TI	Halewood Silver Jubilee 1988
47245	am +	**FE**	DAET	TI	The Institute of Export
47256		**FD**	FDYX	IM (U)	
47258	am +	**FE**	DAET	TI	
47270		**FF**	DFLT	CD	Cory Brothers 1842 – 1992
47276	am +	**FD**	DAET	TI	
47277		**FD**	FDYX	IM (U)	
47278		**FP**	ENXX	SF (U)	
47279		**FF**	DHLT	CD	
47280	am +	**FD**	DAET	TI	Pedigree
47281	am +	**FD**	DAET	TI	
47283		**F**	DFLT	CD	
47284	am +	**FD**	DAXT	TI	
47285	am +	**FE**	DAET	TI	
47286	am +	**FE**	DAET	TI	Port of Liverpool
47287	am +	**FE**	DAET	TI	
47289	a	**F**	DFLT	CD	
47290	am +	**FE**	DFLM	CD	
47291	am +	**FD**	DAYX	TI (U)	
47292	am +	**FD**	DFLM	CD	
47293	am +	**FE**	DAET	TI	
47294	+	**FD**	FDYX	IM (U)	
47295	+	**FP**	LCWX	BS (U)	
47296		**FF**	DFLT	CD	
47297	am +	**FE**	DAET	TI	Cobra RAILFREIGHT
47298	am +	**FD**	DAET	TI	Pegasus
47299	am +	**FE**	DAET	TI	

Class 47/3. Built without Train Heat. (except 47300). RA6. Max. Speed 75 m.p.h. All equipped with slow speed control.

47300		**C**	LCWX	BS (U)	
47301		**FF**	DFLT	CD	Freightliner Birmingham
47302	a	**FR**	DFLT	CD	
47303	am +	**FE**	DFLM	CD	

47304	am +	**FD**	DAET	TI	
47305		**FF**	DFLT	CD	
47306	am +	**FE**	DAET	TI	The Sapper
47307	am +	**FE**	DAET	TI	
47308		**C**	LCWX	BS (U)	
47309	am +	**FD**	DAXT	TI	The Halewood Transmission
47310	am +	**FE**	DAET	TI	Henry Ford
47312	am +	**FE**	DAET	TI	
47313	am +	**FD**	DAET	TI	
47314	am +	**FD**	DAET	TI	Transmark
47315		**C**	ENRN	TO	
47316	am +	**FE**	DAET	TI	
47317		**F**	DFLT	CD	
47319	+	**FP**	FDYX	IM (U)	Norsk Hydro
47322		**FR**	DHLT	CD	
47323	am +	**FE**	DFLM	CD	
47326	am +	**FE**	DAET	TI	Saltley Depot Quality Approved
47328	am +	**FD**	DAET	TI	
47329		**C**	LCWX	BS (U)	
47330	am +	**FD**	DAET	TI	
47331		**C**	FDKI	IM	
47332		**C**	LCWX	BS (U)	
47333		**C**	LCWX	BS (U)	
47334		**C**	LCWX	BS (U)	
47335	am +	**FD**	DAET	TI	
47337		**FF**	DFLM	CD	
47338	am +	**FE**	DAET	TI	
47339		**F**	DFLT	CD	
47340		**C**	DHLT	CD	
47341		**C**	LCWX	BS (U)	
47344	am +	**FE**	DAET	TI	
47345		**FF**	DFLT	CD	
47346		**C**	FDYX	IM (U)	
47347	a	**F**	DFLT	CD	
47348	am	**FE**	DAET	TI	St. Christopher's Railway Home
47349		**F**	DFLT	CD	
47350		**FO**	DFLT	CD	
47351	am +	**FE**	DAET	TI	
47352		**C**	FDYX	IM (U)	
47353		**C**	LCWX	BS (U)	
47354	a	**FF**	DFLT	CD	
47355	am +	**FD**	DAET	TI	
47356		**FO**	DHLT	CD	
47357		**C**	LCXX	BS (U)	
47358		**FF**	DFLT	CD	
47359		**FD**	FDYX	IM (U)	
47360	am +	**FE**	DAET	TI	
47361	am +	**FF**	DFLM	CD	
47362	am +	**FD**	DAET	TI	
47363	am +	**F**	DAET	TI	
47365	am +	**FE**	DAET	TI	ICI Diamond Jubilee

47366	**C**	ENXX	TO (U)	
47367	**FR**	DHLT	CD	
47368	**F**	ENXX	SF (U)	
47369	**FD**	FDYX	IM (U)	
47370	**FE**	DFLT	CD	
47371	**FF**	DFLT	CD	
47372	**C**	LCWX	BS (U)	
47375 am +	**FE**	DAET	TI	Tinsley Traction Depot
				Quality Approved
47376	**FF**	DFLT	CD	Freightliner 1995
47377 a	**F**	DFLT	CD	
47378 am +	**FD**	DAET	TI	
47379 am +	**F**	DAET	TI	

Class 47/4. Equipped with train heating. RA6. Max. Speed 95 m.p.h (§ 75 m.p.h).

47462	**R**	ENXX	SF (U)	
47467	**BR**	PXLD	CD	
47471	**IO**	PXXA	CD (U)	
47473	**BR**	DHLT	CD	
47474 §	**R**	PXLH	CD	Sir Rowland Hill
47475	**RX**	PXLD	CD	Restive
47476	**R**	FDKI	IM	Night Mail
47478		LCWX	BS (U)	
47481	**BR**	PXXA	CD (U)	
47484	**G**	ENXX	SF (U)	ISAMBARD KINGDOM BRUNEL
47488	**W**	PWLS	CD	DAVIES THE OCEAN
47489 §	**R**	PXLH	CD	
47492	**RX**	PXLC	CD	
47501	**R**	PXLD	CD	Craftsman
47513	**BR**	PXLD	CD (S)	Severn
47519 +	**G**	PXLD	CD	
47520	**I**	PXLD	CD	
47522 §	**R**	PXLH	CD	Doncaster Enterprise
47523	**M**	PXLD	CD	
47524	**RX**	PXLD	CD (S)	
47525	**FE**	DAET	TI	
47526	**BR**	ENXX	SF (S)	
47528	**M**	PXLD	CD	The Queen's Own Mercian Yeomanry
47530	**RX**	PXLD	CD (S)	
47532	**RX**	PXLD	CD (S)	
47535	**RX**	PXLD	CD	
47536	**RX**	PXLD	CD (S)	
47539	**RX**	PXXA	CD	
47540	**C**	DAET	TI	The Institution of Civil Engineers
47543	**R**	FDKI	IM	
47547	**N**	PXXA	CD (U)	
47550	**M**	FDYX	IM (U)	University of Dundee
47555	**FE**	DAYX	TI	The Commonwealth Spirit
47565	**RX**	PXLC	CD	Responsive
47566	**RX**	PXLD	CD (U)	

47572	**R** PXLC	CD	Ely Cathedral
47574	**R** FDKI	IM	Benjamin Gimbert G.C.
47575	**R** PXLC	CD	City of Hereford
47576	**RX** PXLD	CD (S)	
47584	**RX** PXLC	CD	THE LOCOMOTIVE & CARRIAGE INSTITUTION
47596	**RX** PXLC	CD	
47624	**RX** PXLC	CD	Saint Andrew
47627	**RX** PXLC	CD	
47628 j	**RX** PXLC	CD	
47634	**R** PXLC	CD	Holbeck
47635 j	**R** PXLC	CD	
47640 j	**R** PXLC	CD	University of Strathclyde

Class 47/6. Fitted with high phosphorus brake blocks. RA6. Max. Speed 75 m.p.h.

| 47676 | **I** FDYX | IM (U) | |
| 47677 | **I** FDYX | IM (U) | |

Class 47/7. Fitted with an older form of TDM. RA6. Max. Speed 95 m.p.h. All have twin fuel tanks.

47701	**RX** PWLS	CD	
47702	**F** ENRN	TO	County of Suffolk
47703	**W** PWLS	CD	LEWIS CARROLL
47704	**RX** PXLD	CD	
47705	**W** PWLS	CD	GUY FAWKES
47709	**RX** PWLS	CD	
47710	**W** PWLO	CD	
47711	**N** ENXX	TO (U)	County of Hertfordshire
47712	**W** PWLO	CD	DICK WHITTINGTON
47715	**N** PXLD	CD (S)	Haymarket
47716	**RX** PXLD	CD (S)	
47717	**R** PXXA	CD (U) \	

Class 47/7. Parcels dedicated locos. RA6. Max. Speed 95 m.p.h. All have twin fuel tanks and are fitted with RCH jumper cables for operating with propelling control vehicles (PCVs).

47721 (47557)	**RX** PXLB	CD	Saint Bede
47722 (47558) a	**RX** PXLB	CD	The Queen Mother
47725 (47567)	**RX** PXLB	CD	The Railway Mission
47726 (47568)	**RX** PXLB	CD	Progress
47727 (47569) a	**RX** PXLB	CD	Duke of Edinburgh's Award
47732 (47580)	**RX** PXLB	CD	Restormel
47733 (47582) a	**RX** PXLB	CD	Eastern Star
47734 (47583)	**RX** PXLB	CD	Crewe Diesel Depot Quality Approved
47736 (47587) a	**RX** PXLB	CD	Cambridge Traction & Rolling Stock Depot
47737 (47588)	**RX** PXLB	CD	Resurgent
47738 (47592) a	**RX** PXLB	CD	Bristol Barton Hill
47739 (47594) a	**RX** PXLB	CD	Resourceful

47741 (47597)		**RX** PXLB	CD	Resilient
47742 (47598)		**RX** PXLB	CD	The Enterprising Scot
47744 (47600)	a	**RX** PXLB	CD	Saint Edwin
47745 (47603)		**RX** PXLB	CD	Royal London Society for the Blind
47746 (47605)	a	**RX** PXLB	CD	The Bobby
47747 (47615)	a	**RX** PXLB	CD	Res Publica
47749 (47625)		**RX** PXLB	CD	Atlantic College
47750 (47626)	a	**RX** PXLB	CD	Royal Mail Cheltenham
47756 (47644)		**RX** PXLB	CD	Royal Mail Tyneside
47757 (47585)	a	**RX** PXLB	CD	Restitution
47758 (47517)		**RX** PXLB	CD	
47759 (47559)		**RX** PXLB	CD	
47760 (47562)		**RX** PXLB	CD	Restless
47761 (47564)		**RX** PXLB	CD	
47762 (47573)		**RX** PXLB	CD	
47763 (47581)		**RX** PXLB	CD	
47764 (47630)		**RX** PXLB	CD	Resounding
47765 (47631)		**RX** PXLB	CD	Ressaldar
47766 (47642)		**RX** PXLB	CD	Resolute
47767 (47641)		**RX** PXLB	CD	Saint Columba
47768 (47490)		**RX** PXLB	CD	Resonant
47769 (47491)		**RX** PXLB	CD	Resolve
47770 (47500)		**RX** PXLB	CD	Reserved
47771 (47503)		**RX** PXLB	CD	Heaton Traincare Depot
47772 (47537)		**RX** PXLB	CD	
47773 (47541)		**RX** PXLB	CD	Reservist
47774 (47551)		**RX** PXLB	CD	Poste Restante
47775 (47531)		**RX** PXLB	CD	Respite
47776 (47578)		**RX** PXLB	CD	Respected
47777 (47636)		**RX** PXLB	CD	Restored
47778 (47606)		**RX** PXLB	CD	Irresistible
47779 (47612)		**RX** PXLB	CD	
47780 (47618)		**RX** PXLB	CD	
47781 (47653)		**RX** PXLB	CD	Isle of Iona
47782 (47824)		**RX** PXLB	CD	
47783 (47809)		**RX** PXLB	CD	Saint Peter
47784 (47819)		**RX** PXLB	CD	Condover Hall
47785 (47820)		**RX** PXLB	CD	The Statesman
47786 (47821)	a	**RX** PXLB	CD	Roy Castle OBE
47787 (47823)		**RX** PXLB	CD	Victim Support
47788 (47833)	a	**RX** PXLB	CD	Captain Peter Manisty RN
47789 (47616)	a	**RX** PXLB	CD	Lindisfarne
47790 (47673)	a	**RX** PXLB	CD	Saint David/Dewi Sant
47791 (47675)	a	**RX** PXLB	CD	VENICE SIMPLON ORIENT EXPRESS
47792 (47804)		**RX** PXLB	CD	Saint Cuthbert
47793 (47579)		**RX** PXLB	CD	Saint Augustine

Class 47/4 continued. RA6. Max. Speed 95 m.p.h.

47798 a	**0**	PXLP	CD	Prince William
47799 a	**0**	PXLP	CD	Prince Henry
47802 +	**I**	ENXX	SF (S)	
47803 +	**0**	ENXX	SF (S)	
47805 a+	**I**	ILRA	CD	
47806 a+	**I**	ILRA	CD	
47807 a+	**PL**	ILRB	CD	
47810 a+	**I**	ILRA	CD	PORTERBROOK
47811 a+	**I**	IWLX	LA	
47812 a+	**I**	ILRA	CD	
47813 a+	**I**	IWLX	LA	
47814 a+	**I**	ILRA	CD	
47815 a+	**I**	IWLA	LA	
47816 a+	**I**	IWLA	LA	Bristol Bath Road Quality Approved
47817 a+	**PL**	ILRB	CD	
47818 a+	**I**	ILRA	CD	
47822 a+	**I**	ILRA	CD	
47825 a+	**I**	ILRA	CD	Thomas Telford
47826 a+	**I**	ILRA	CD	
47827 a+	**I**	ILRA	CD	
47828 a+	**I**	ILRA	CD	
47829 a+	**I**	ILRA	CD	
47830 a+	**I**	IWLX	LA	
47831 a+	**I**	ILRA	CD	Bolton Wanderer
47832 a+	**I**	IWLA	LA	
47839 a+	**I**	ILRA	CD	
47840 a+	**I**	ILRA	CD	NORTH STAR
47841 a+	**I**	ILRA	CD	The Institution of
				Mechanical Engineers
47843 a+	**I**	ILRA	CD	
47844 a+	**I**	ILRA	CD	Derby & Derbyshire Chamber
				of Commerce & Industry
47845 a+	**I**	IWLX	LA	County of Kent
47846 a+	**U**	IWLA	LA	THOR
47847 a+	**I**	ILRA	CD	
47848 a+	**I**	ILRA	CD	
47849 a+	**I**	ILRA	CD	
47851 a+	**I**	ILRA	CD	
47853 a+	**I**	ILRA	CD	
47854 a+	**I**	ILRA	CD	Women's Royal Voluntary Service
47971 *	**BR**	PXLK	CD	Robin Hood
47972	**CS**	PXLD	CD	The Royal Army Ordnance Corps
47976 *	**C**	PXLK	CD	Aviemore Centre

Class 47/3 continued. RA6. Max. Speed 75 m.p.h.

47981	**C**	FDKI	IM

CLASS 55   DELTIC   Co–Co

Built: 1961 by English Electric, Vulcan Foundry.
Engines: Two Napier Deltic T18-25 of 1230 kW (1650 h.p.) at 1500 rpm.
Main Generators: Two English Electric EE829.
Traction Motors: EE538 (axle hung).
Max. Tractive Effort: 222 kN (50000 lbf).
Cont. Tractive Effort: 136 kN (30500 lbf) at 32.5 m.p.h.
Power At Rail: 1969 kW (2640 hp).   **Length over Buffers:** 17.65 m.
Brake Force: 51 t.   **Wheel Diameter:** 1092 mm.
Design Speed: 100 m.p.h.   **Weight:** 105 t.
Max. Speed: 90 m.p.h.   **RA:** 5.
Train Brakes: Air & vacuum.   **Multiple Working:** Not equipped.
ETH Index: 66.

Owned by 9000 locomotives Ltd.

Carries original number D 9000.

| 55022 | **G** | | BN | ROYAL SCOTS GREY |

CLASS 56   BRUSH TYPE 5   Co–Co

Built: 1976 – 84 by Electroputere at Craiova, Romania (as sub contractors for Brush) or BREL at Doncaster or Crewe Works.
Engine: Ruston Paxman 16RK3CT of 2460 kW (3250 hp) at 900 rpm.
Main Alternator: Brush BA1101A.
Traction Motors: Brush TM73-62.
Max. Tractive Effort: 275 kN (61800 lbf).
Cont. Tractive Effort: 240 kN (53950 lbf) at 16.8 m.p.h.
Power At Rail: 1790 kW (2400 hp).   **Length over Buffers:** 19.36 m.
Brake Force: 60 t.   **Wheel Diameter:** 1143 mm.
Design Speed: 80 m.p.h.   **Weight:** 125 t.
Max. Speed: 80 m.p.h.   **RA:** 7.
Train Brakes: Air.
Multiple Working: Red Diamond coupling code.
Communication Equipment: Cab to shore radio-telephone.
All equipped with slow speed control.

56001	**FA**	LCYX	CF (U)	
56003	**LH**	FMBY	TE	
56004		LWBK	IM	
56006	**LH**	FMBY	TE	Ferrybridge 'C' Power Station
56007	**FT**	LWBK	IM	
56008		FDYX	IM (U)	
56010	**FT**	LNBK	CF	
56011	**F**	FDYX	IM (U)	
56012	**FC**	FDYX	IM (U)	
56014	**FC**	FDYX	IM (U)	
56018	**FT**	LNBK	CF	
56019	**FR**	LCWX	CF (U)	
56020		LCWX	CF (U)	

56021	LH	FDBI	IM	
56022	FT	LWBK	IM	
56025	FT	LWBK	IM	
56027	LH	FDBK	IM	
56029	F	LWBK	IM	
56031	C	FMBY	TE	
56032	FS	LNBK	CF	Sir De Morgannwg/ County of South Glamorgan
56033	FT	LWBK	IM	Shotton Paper Mill
56034	LH	FDBK	IM	Castell Ogwr/Ogmore Castle
56035	LH	FMBY	TE	
56036	CT	LWBK	IM	
56037	FT	LCWX	CF (S)	Richard Trevithick
56038	FT	FDBK	IM	Western Mail
56039	LH	FMBY	TE	ABP Port of Hull
56040	FT	LNBK	CF	Oystermouth
56041	U	FDBI	IM	
56043	FS	FDBK	IM	
56044	FT	LNBK	CF	Cardiff Canton Quality Assured
56045	LH	FMBY	TE	
56046	C	FMBY	TE	
56047	CT	LWBK	IM	
56048	C	FMBY	TE	
56049	CT	LWBK	IM	
56050	LH	FMBY	TE	British Steel Teeside
56051	EW	FDBK	IM	Isle of Grain
56052	FT	LNBK	CF	
56053	FT	LNBK	CF	Sir Morgannwg Ganol/ County of Mid Glamorgan
56054	FT	LWBK	IM	British Steel Llanwern
56055	LH	FDBI	IM	
56056	FT	LGAM	ML	
56057	EW	LGAM	ML	British Fuels
56058	EW	LGAM	ML	
56059	FA	LWBK	IM	
56060	FT	LCWX	CF (U)	The Cardiff.Rod Mill
56061	FS	FMBY	TE	
56062	F	FMBY	TE	Mountsorrel
56063	F	FMBY	TE	Bardon Hill
56064	FT	LNBK	CF	
56065	FA	FMBY	TE	
56066	FT	LWBK	IM	
56067	EW	FDBK	IM	
56068	U	FDBI	IM	
56069	FS	FMBY	TE	Thornaby TMD
56070	FT	LWBK	IM	
56071	FT	LWBK	IM	
56072	FT	LGAM	ML	
56073	FT	LNBK	CF	Tremorfa Steelworks
56074	LH	FMBY	TE	Kellingley Colliery
56075	F	FDBK	IM	West Yorkshire Enterprise

56076	FS	LNBK	CF	
56077	LH	FDBI	IM	Thorpe Marsh Power Station
56078	F	FDBK	IM	
56079	FT	LGAM	ML	
56080	F	FDBK	IM	Selby Coalfield
56081	F	FMBY	TE	
56082	F	FDBK	IM	
56083	LH	FDBK	IM	
56084	LH	FMBY	TE	
56085	LH	FDBK	IM	
56086	FT	LWBK	IM	The Magistrates' Association
56087	FS	FDBK	IM	
56088	EW	FDBK	IM	
56089	EW	FDBI	IM	
56090	LH	FDBI	IM	
56091	F	FDBK	IM	Castle Donington Power Station
56092	FT	LWBK	IM	
56093	FT	LWBK	IM	The Institution of Mining Engineers
56094	FC	FDBK	IM	Eggborough Power Station
56095	F	FMBY	TE	Harworth Colliery
56096	EW	LWBK	IM	
56097	FS	FMBY	TE	
56098	F	FMBY	TE	
56099	FT	LWBK	IM	Fiddlers Ferry Power Station
56100	LH	FDBI	IM	
56101	FT	LWBK	IM	Mutual Improvement
56102	LH	FDBI	IM	Scunthorpe Steel Centenary
56103	FT	LNBK	CF	
56104	FC	LGAM	ML	
56105	EW	LWBK	IM	
56106	LH	FDBI	IM	
56107	LH	FDBI	IM	
56108	F	FMBY	TE	
56109	LH	FDBI	IM	
56110	LH	FMBY	TE	Croft
56111	LH	FDBI	IM	
56112	LH	FMBY	TE	Stainless Pioneer
56113	FT	LNBK	CF	
56114	EW	LCWX	CF	Maltby Colliery
56115	FT	LNBK	CF	
56116	LH	FDBI	IM	
56117	FC	FMBY	TE	Wilton-Coalpower
56118	LH	FDBI	IM	
56119	FT	LNBK	CF	
56120	EW	FDBI	IM	
56121	FC	LNBK	CF	
56123	FT	LGAM	ML	Drax Power Station
56124	FC	LGAM	ML	
56125	FT	LWBK	IM	
56126	FC	FDBK	IM	
56127	FT	LWBK	IM	

56128	FC	LGAM	ML	
56129	FT	LGAM	ML	
56130	LH	FMBY	TE	Wardley Opencast
56131	F	FDBK	IM	Ellington Colliery
56132	FT	LWBK	IM	
56133	FT	LWBK	IM	Crewe Locomotive Works
56134	FC	FMBY	TE	Blyth Power
56135	F	FDBK	IM	Port of Tyne Authority

CLASS 58   BREL TYPE 5   Co – Co

Built: 1983 – 87 by BREL at Doncaster Works.
Engine: Ruston Paxman RK3ACT of 2460 kW (3300 hp) at 1000 rpm.
Main Alternator: Brush BA1101B.
Traction Motors: Brush TM73-62.
Max. Tractive Effort: 275 kN (61800 lbf).
Cont. Tractive Effort: 240 kN (53950 lbf) at 17.4 m.p.h.
Power At Rail: 1780 kW (2387 hp). **Length over Buffers:** 19.13 m.
Brake Force: 62 t.   **Wheel Diameter:** 1120 mm.
Design Speed: 80 m.p.h.   **Weight:** 130 t.
Max. Speed: 80 m.p.h.   **RA:** 7.
Train Brakes: Air.
Multiple Working: Red Diamond coupling code.
Communication Equipment: Cab to shore radio-telephone.
All equipped with slow speed control.

58001	FM	ENBN	TO	
58002	ML	ENBN	TO	Daw Mill Colliery
58003	FM	ENBN	TO	Markham Colliery
58004	FM	ENBN	TO	
58005	ML	ENBN	TO	Ironbridge Power Station
58006	F	ENBN	TO	
58007	FM	ENBN	TO	Drakelow Power Station
58008	ML	ENBN	TO	
58009	FM	ENBN	TO	
58010	FM	ENBN	TO	
58011	FM	ENBN	TO	Worksop Depot
58012	FM	ENBN	TO	
58013	ML	ENBN	TO	
58014	ML	ENBN	TO	Didcot Power Station
58015	FM	ENBN	TO	
58016	EW	ENBN	TO	
58017	FM	ENBN	TO	Eastleigh Depot
58018	FM	ENBN	TO	High Marnham Power Station
58019	FM	ENBN	TO	Shirebrook Colliery
58020	FM	ENBN	TO	Doncaster Works
58021	ML	ENBN	TO	Hither Green Depot
58022	FM	ENBN	TO	
58023	ML	ENBN	TO	Peterborough Depot
58024	EW	ENBN	TO	
58025	FM	ENBN	TO	

58026	FM	ENBN	TO	
58027	FM	ENBN	TO	
58028	FM	ENBN	TO	
58029	FM	ENBN	TO	
58030	FM	ENBN	TO	
58031	FM	ENBN	TO	
58032	ML	ENBN	TO	Thoresby Colliery
58033	EW	ENBN	TO	
58034	FM	ENBN	TO	Bassetlaw
58035	FM	ENBN	TO	
58036	ML	ENBN	TO	
58037	FM	ENBN	TO	
58038	ML	ENBN	TO	
58039	FM	ENBN	TO	Rugeley Power Station
58040	FM	ENBN	TO	Cottam Power Station
58041	FM	ENBN	TO	Ratcliffe Power Station
58042	ML	ENBN	TO	Petrolea
58043	FM	ENBN	TO	
58044	FM	ENBN	TO	Oxcroft Opencast
58045	FM	ENBN	TO	
58046	ML	ENBN	TO	Asfordby Mine
58047	FM	ENBN	TO	Manton Colliery
58048	EW	ENBN	TO	
58049	EW	ENBN	TO	Littleton Colliery
58050	ML	ENBN	TO	Toton Traction Depot

CLASS 59   GENERAL MOTORS TYPE 5   Co – Co

Built: 1985 (59001 – 4), 1989 (59005) by General Motors, La Grange, Illinois, U.S.A. or 1990 (59101 – 4), 1994 (59201) and 1995 (59202 – 6) by General Motors, London, Ontario, Canada.
Engine: General Motors 645E3C two stroke of 2460 kW (3300 hp) at 900 rpm.
Main Alternator: General Motors AR11 MLD-D14A.
Traction Motors: General Motors D77B.
Max. Tractive Effort: 506 kN (113 550 lbf).
Cont. Tractive Effort: 291 kN (65 300 lbf) at 14.3 m.p.h.
Power At Rail: 1889 kW (2533 hp).   **Length over Buffers:** 21.35 m.
Brake Force: 69 t.   **Wheel Diameter:** 1067 mm.
Weight: 121 t.   **RA:** 7.
Design Speed: 60 m.p.h. (75 m.p.h Cl. 59/2).
Max. Speed: 60 m.p.h. (75 m.p.h. Cl. 59/2).

Class 59/0. Owned by Foster-Yeoman Ltd. Blue/silver/blue livery with white lettering and cast numberplates.

59001	0	XYPO	MD	YEOMAN ENDEAVOUR
59002	0	XYPO	MD	ALAN J DAY
59003	0	XYPO	MD	YEOMAN HIGHLANDER
59004	0	XYPO	MD	PAUL A HAMMOND
59005	0	XYPO	MD	KENNETH J. PAINTER

Class 59/1. Owned by ARC Limited. Yellow/grey with grey lettering and cast numberplates.

59101	**0**	XYPA	WH	Village of Whatley
59102	**0**	XYPA	WH	Village of Chantry
59103	**0**	XYPA	WH	Village of Mells
59104	**0**	XYPA	WH	Village of Great Elm

Class 59/2. Owned by National Power. Grey, red, white and blue with white and red lettering and cast numberplates.

59201	**0**	XYPN	FB	Vale of York
59202	**0**	XYPN	FB	Vale of White Horse
59203	**0**	XYPN	FB	Vale of Pickering
59204	**0**	XYPN	FB	Vale of Glamorgan
59205	**0**	XYPN	FB	Vale of Evesham
59206	**0**	XYPN	FB	

CLASS 60   BRUSH TYPE 5   Co – Co

Built: 1989 – 1993 by Brush Traction at Loughborough.
Engine: Mirrlees MB275T of 2310 kW (3100 hp) at 1000 rpm.
Main Alternator: Brush .
Traction Motors: Brush separately excited.
Max. Tractive Effort: 500 kN (106500 lbf).
Cont. Tractive Effort: 336 kN (71570 lbf) at 17.4 m.p.h.
Power At Rail: 1800 kW (2415 hp).   **Length over Buffers:** 21.34 m.
Brake Force: 74 t.   **Wheel Diameter:** 1118 mm.
Design Speed: 62 m.p.h.   **Weight:** 129 t (130 t +).
Max. Speed: 60 m.p.h.   **RA:** 7.
Multiple Working: Within class.
Communication Equipment: Cab to shore radio-telephone.
All equipped with slow speed control.

60001		**FA**	ENAN	SL
60002	+	**FP**	FDAI	IM	Capability Brown
60003		**FP**	FDAI	IM	Christopher Wren
60004	+	**EW**	FMAY	TE	
60005		**FT**	LWAK	TO	Skiddaw
60006		**FM**	ENAN	TO	Great Gable
60007	+	**LH**	FDAI	IM	
60008		**LH**	FMAY	TE	GYPSUM QUEEN II
60009	+	**FM**	ENAN	TO	Carnedd Dafydd
60010		**FM**	ENAN	TO	Pumlumon Plynlimon
60011		**ML**	ENAN	TO	Cader Idris
60012	+	**EW**	ENAN	TO	
60013		**FP**	FDAI	IM	Robert Boyle
60014		**EW**	FDAI	IM	
60015	+	**FT**	LNAK	CF	Bow Fell
60016		**FA**	LNAK	CF	Langdale Pikes
60017	+	**EW**	ENAN	TO	Shotton Works Centenary Year 1996
60018		**FM**	ENAN	SL	Moel Siabod
60019		**EW**	ENAN	SL	

60020	+	FS	FMAY	TE	Great Whernside
60021	+	FS	FDAI	IM	Pen-y-Ghent
60022	+	U	FDAI	IM	
60023		FS	FMAY	TE	The Cheviot
60024		EW	FDAI	IM	
60025	+	LH	FDAI	IM	
60026	+	EW	FDAI	IM	
60027	+	EW	FDAI	IM	
60028	+	FP	FDAI	IM	John Flamsteed
60029		FT	LNAK	CF	Ben Nevis
60030		FS	FMAY	TE	Cir Mhor
60031		FS	FMAY	TE	Ben Lui
60032		FT	LWAK	TO	William Booth
60033		FT	LNAK	CF	Anthony Ashley Cooper
60034		FT	LNAK	CF	Carnedd Llewelyn
60035		FT	LNAK	CF	Florence Nightingale
60036		FT	LNAK	CF	Sgurr Na Ciche
60037		FT	LNAK	CF	Helvellyn
60038	+	LH	FDAI	IM	
60039		FM	ENAN	SL	Glastonbury Tor
60040		EW	ENAN	SL	
60041	+	FM	ENAN	SL	
60042		FM	ENAN	SL	Dunkery Beacon
60043		FM	ENAN	SL	Yes Tor
60044		ML	ENAN	TO	Ailsa Craig
60045		FT	LWAK	TO	Josephine Butler
60046		FT	LWAK	TO	William Wilberforce
60047	+	EW	LWAK	TO	
60048		EW	ENAN	TO	
60049		FS	FMAY	TE	Scafell
60050		EW	FMAY	TE	
60051		FP	FDAI	IM	Mary Somerville
60052		FS	FMAY	TE	Goat Fell
60053		FP	FMAY	TE	John Reith
60054	+	FP	FDAI	IM	Charles Babbage
60055		FT	LWAK	TO	Thomas Barnardo
60056		FT	LWAK	TO	William Beveridge
60057		FC	LWAK	TO	Adam Smith
60058		FT	LWAK	TO	John Howard
60059	+	LH	FDAI	IM	Swinden Dalesman
60060		FC	LWAK	TO	James Watt
60061		FT	LWAK	TO	Alexander Graham Bell
60062		FT	LNAK	CF	Samuel Johnson
60063		FT	LNAK	CF	James Murray
60064	+	FL	FDAI	IM	Back Tor
60065		FT	LNAK	CF	Kinder Low
60066		FT	LWAK	TO	John Logie Baird
60067		F	FDAI	IM	James Clerk-Maxwell
60068		F	FMAY	TE	Charles Darwin
60069		F	FMAY	TE	Humphry Davy
60070	+	FL	FDAI	IM	John Loudon McAdam

60071	+	FM	ENAN	TO	Dorothy Garrod
60072		FM	ENAN	TO	Cairn Toul
60073		FM	ENAN	TO	Cairn Gorm
60074		FM	ENAN	TO	Braeriach
60075		FM	ENAN	TO	Liathach
60076		FM	ENAN	TO	Suilven
60077	+	FM	ENAN	TO	Canisp
60078		ML	ENAN	TO	
60079		FM	ENAN	TO	Foinaven
60080	+	FT	LNAK	CF	Kinder Scout
60081		FT	LNAK	CF	Bleaklow Hill
60082		FA	LNAK	CF	Mam Tor
60083		FM	LNAK	TO	Shining Tor
60084		FT	LNAK	CF	Cross Fell
60085		FT	LWAK	TO	Axe Edge
60086		FM	ENAN	TO	Schiehallion
60087		FM	ENAN	TO	Slioch
60088		FM	ENAN	TO	Buachaille Etive Mor
60089		FT	LNAK	CF	Arcuil
60090	+	FC	FDAI	IM	Quinag
60091		FC	FDAI	IM	An Teallach
60092		FT	LNAK	CF	Reginald Munns
60093		FT	LNAK	CF	Jack Stirk
60094		FM	ENAN	TO	Tryfan
60095		FA	LWAK	TO	Crib Goch
60096		FT	LNAK	CF	Ben Macdui
60097		FT	LWAK	TO	Pillar
60098		FM	ENAN	TO	Charles Francis Brush
60099		FM	ENAN	SL	Ben More Assynt
60100		FM	ENAN	SL	Boar of Badenoch

2. ELECTRIC LOCOMOTIVES

CLASS 73/0   ELECTRO – DIESEL   Bo – Bo

Built: 1962 by BR at Eastleigh Works.
Supply System: 660 – 850 V d.c. from third rail.
Engine: English Electric 4SRKT of 447 kW (600 hp) at 850 rpm.
Main Generator: English Electric 824/3D.
Traction Motors: English Electric 542A.
Max. Tractive Effort: Electric 187 kN (42000 lbf). Diesel 152 kN (34100 lbf).
Continuous Rating: Electric 1060 kW (1420 hp) giving a tractive effort of 43 kN (9600 lbf) at 55.5 mph.
Cont. Tractive Effort: Diesel 72 kN (16100 lbf) at 10 mph.
Maximum Rail Power: Electric 1830 kW (2450 hp) at 37 mph.

Brake Force: 31 t.	**Length over Buffers:** 16.36 m.
Design Speed: 80 m.p.h.	**Weight:** 76.5 t.
Max. Speed: 60 m.p.h.	**RA:** 6.
Wheel Diameter: 1016 mm.	**ETH Index (Elec. power):** 66

Train Brakes: Air, Vacuum and electro-pneumatic.
Multiple Working: Within sub-class, with Class 33/1 and various 750 V d.c. EMUs.
Communication Equipment: All equipped with driver – guard telephone.
Couplings: Drop-head buckeye.

Non-standard Livery: 73005 is Network SouthEast blue.

Formerly numbered E 6002/5.

73002	**BR** HEBD	BD (U)	
73005	**0** HEBD	BD (U)	

CLASS 73/1 & 73/2   ELECTRO – DIESEL   Bo – Bo

Built: 1965 – 67 by English Electric Co. at Vulcan Foundry, Newton le Willows.
Supply System: 660 – 850 V d.c. from third rail.
Engine: English Electric 4SRKT of 447 kW (600 hp) at 850 rpm.
Main Generator: English Electric 824/5D.
Traction Motors: English Electric 546/1B.
Max. Tractive Effort: Electric 179 kN (40000 lbf). Diesel 160 kN (36000 lbf).
Continuous Rating: Electric 1060 kW (1420 hp) giving a tractive effort of 35 kN (7800 lbf) at 68 mph.
Cont. Tractive Effort: Diesel 60 kN (13600 lbf) at 11.5 mph.
Maximum Rail Power: Electric 2350 kW (3150 hp) at 42 mph.

Brake Force: 31 t.	**Length over Buffers:** 16.36 m.
Design Speed: 90 m.p.h.	**Weight:** 77 t.
Max. Speed: 60 (90*) m.p.h.	**RA:** 6.
Wheel Diameter: 1016 mm.	**ETH Index (Elec. power):** 66

Train Brakes: Air, Vacuum and electro-pneumatic.
Multiple Working: Within sub-class, with Class 33/1 and various 750 V d.c. EMUs.
Communication Equipment: All equipped with driver – guard telephone.

Couplings: Drop-head buckeye.

a Vacuum brake isolated.

Formerly numbered E 6001 – 20/22 – 26/28 – 49 (not in order).

IVGA locos are owned by Porterbrook Leasing Company.
73109 is owned by Stagecoach Ltd.
73118/30 are owned by Eurostar (GB) Ltd.

73101	**EW**	EWEB	SL
73103	**IO**	EWEB	SL
73104	**IO**	EWEB	SL
73105	**C**	EWEB	SL
73106	**D**	EWEB	SL
73107	**C**	EWEB	SL	Redhill 1844 – 1994
73108	**C**	EWEB	SL
73109 *	**SC**	HYSB	BM	Battle of Britain 50th Anniversary
73110	**C**	EWEB	SL
73114	**ML**	EWEB	SL	Stewarts Lane
Traction Maintenance Depot
73117	**IO**	EWEB	SL	University of Surrey
73118 c	**E**	GPSN	SL
73119	**C**	EWEB	SL	Kentish Mercury
73126	**N**	ENXX	SL (U)	Kent & East Sussex Railway
73128	**EW**	EWRB	SL
73129	**N**	EWEB	SL	City of Winchester
73130 c	**E**	GPSN	SL
73131	**EW**	EWRB	SL
73132	**IO**	EWRB	SL
73133	**ML**	EWEB	SL	The Bluebell Railway
73134	**IO**	EWEB	SL	Woking Homes 1885 – 1985
73136	**ML**	EWEB	SL	Kent Youth Music
73138	**C**	EWEB	SL
73139	**IO**	EWRB	SL
73140	**IO**	EWRB	SL
73141	**IO**	EWRB	SL
73201 a*	**GE**	IVGA	SL	Broadlands
73202 a*	**GE**	IVGA	SL	Royal Observer Corps
73203 a*	**GE**	IVGA	SL
73204 a*	**GE**	IVGA	SL	Stewarts Lane 1860 – 1985
73205 a*	**GE**	IVGA	SL
73206 a*	**GE**	IVGA	SL	Gatwick Express
73207 a*	**GE**	IVGA	SL	County of East Sussex
73208 a*	**GE**	IVGA	SL	Croydon 1883 – 1983
73209 a*	**GE**	IVGA	SL
73210 a*	**GE**	IVGA	SL	Selhurst
73211 a*	**GE**	IVGA	SL
73212 a*	**GE**	IVGA	SL	Airtour Suisse
73213 a*	**GE**	IVGA	SL	University of Kent at Canterbury
73235 a*	**GE**	IVGA	SL

CLASS 73/9   ELECTRO – DIESEL   Bo – Bo

For details see Class 73/0. Sandite fitted locos.

Formerly numbered E 6001/6.

| 73901 | (73001) | **MD** HEBD | BD |
| 73906 | (73006) | **MD** HEBD | BD |

NOTES FOR CLASSES 86 – 91.

The following common features apply to all locos of Classes 86 – 91.
Supply System: 25 kV a.c. from overhead equipment.
Communication Equipment: Driver – guard telephone and cab to shore radio-telephone.
Multiple Working: Time division multiplex system (87101 not fitted).

a vacuum brakes isolated.

Class 86 were formerly numbered E 3101 – 3200 (not in order).

CLASS 86/1   BR DESIGN   Bo – Bo

Built: 1965 – 66 by English Electric Co. at Vulcan Foundry, Newton le Willows or BR at Doncaster Works. Rebuilt with Class 87 type bogies and motors. Tap changer control.
Traction Motors: GEC G412AZ frame mounted.
Max. Tractive Effort: 258 kN (58000 lbf).
Continuous Rating: 3730 kW (5000 hp) giving a tractive effort of 95 kN (21300 lbf) at 87 mph.
Maximum Rail Power: 5860 kW (7860 hp) at 50.8 mph.

Brake Force: 40 t.	**Length over Buffers:** 17.83 m.
Design Speed: 110 m.p.h.	**Weight:** 87 t.
Max. Speed: 110 m.p.h.	**RA:** 6.
ETH Index: 74	**Wheel Diameter:** 1150 mm.
Train Brakes: Air & Vacuum.	**Electric Brake:** Rheostatic.

Owned by Eversholt Train Leasing Company.

86101	I	IWPA	WN	Sir William A Stanier FRS
86102 a	I	IWPA	WN	Robert A Riddles
86103	I	SAXL	WN	André Chapelon

CLASS 86/2   BR DESIGN   Bo – Bo

Built: 1965 – 66 by English Electric Co. at Vulcan Foundry, Newton le Willows or BR at Doncaster Works. Later rebuilt with resilient wheels and flexicoil suspension. Tap changer control.
Traction Motors: AEI 282BZ.
Max. Tractive Effort: 207 kN (46500 lbf).
Continuous Rating: 3010 kW (4040 hp) giving a tractive effort of 85 kN (19200 lbf) at 77.5 mph.
Maximum Rail Power: 4550 kW (6100 hp) at 49.5 mph.

Brake Force: 40 t.
Design Speed: 125 m.p.h.
Max. Speed: 100 (110§) m.p.h.
ETH Index: 66
Train Brakes: Air & Vacuum.

Length over Buffers: 17.83 m.
Weight: 85 t – 86 t.
RA: 6.
Wheel Diameter: 1156 mm.
Electric Brake: Rheostatic.

Owned by Eversholt Train Leasing Company (except for PXLE locos which are owned by English Welsh & Scottish Railway).

86204		I	IANA	NC	City of Carlisle
86205	a	I	ICCA	LG	City of Lancaster
86206	a	I	ICCA	LG	City of Stoke on Trent
86207	a	I	IWPA	WN	City of Lichfield
86208	a	I	PXLE	CE	City of Chester
86209	a§	I	IWPA	WN	City of Coventry
86210		RX	PXLE	CE	C.I.T. 75th Anniversary
86212		I	ICCA	LG	Preston Guild 1328 – 1992
86213		I	SAXL	LG	Lancashire Witch
86214		I	ICCA	LG	Sans Pareil
86215	a	I	IANA	NC	Norwich Cathedral
86216	a	I	ICCA	LG	Meteor
86217	a	I	IANA	NC	City University
86218		I	IANA	NC	Harold MacMillan
86219	a	I	SAXL	WN (S)	Phoenix
86220	a	I	IANA	NC	The Round Tabler
86221	a	I	IANA	NC	B.B.C. Look East
86222		I	ICCA	LG	Clothes Show Live
86223	a	I	IANA	NC	Norwich Union
86224	a§	I	IWPA	WN	Caledonian
86225	a§	I	IWPA	WN	Hardwicke
86226		I	ICCA	LG	CHARLES RENNIE MACKINTOSH
86227	a	I	ICCA	LG	Sir Henry Johnson
86228		I	IANA	NC	Vulcan Heritage
86229		I	ICCA	LG	Sir John Betjeman
86230	a	I	IANA	NC	The Duke of Wellington
86231	a§	I	IWPA	WN	Starlight Express
86232	a	I	IANA	NC	Norfolk and Norwich Festival
86233		I	ICCA	LG	Laurence Olivier
86234		I	ICCA	LG	J B Priestley OM
86235	a	I	IANA	NC	Crown Point
86236	a	I	IWPA	WN	Josiah Wedgwood
					MASTER POTTER 1736 – 1795
86237	a	I	IANA	NC	University of East Anglia
86238	a	I	IANA	NC	European Community
86240	a	I	IWPA	WN	Bishop Eric Treacy
86241		RX	PXLE	CE	Glenfiddich
86242		I	IWPA	WN	James Kennedy GC
86243		RX	PXLE	CE	
86244		I	ICCA	LG	The Royal British Legion
86245	a	I	IWPA	WN	Dudley Castle
86246	a	I	IANA	NC	Royal Anglian Regiment
86247	a	I	ICCA	LG	Abraham Darby

86248		I	IWPA	WN	Sir Clwyd/County of Clwyd
86249	a	I	SAXL	WN (S)	County of Merseyside
86250	a	I	IANA	NC	The Glasgow Herald
86251		I	IWPA	WN	The Birmingham Post
86252		I	ICCA	LG	The Liverpool Daily Post
86253	a	I	IWPA	WN	The Manchester Guardian
86254		RX	PXLE	CE	
86255		I	ICCA	LG	Penrith Beacon
86256		I	IWPA	WN	Pebble Mill
86257	a	I	IANA	NC	Snowdon
86258	a	I	IWPA	WN	Talyllyn – The First Preserved Railway
86259	a	I	ICCA	LG	Greater MANCHESTER THE LIFE & SOUL OF BRITAIN
86260	a	I	ICCA	LG	Driver Wallace Oakes G.C.
86261		RX	PXLE	CE	

CLASS 86/4 & 86/6   BR DESIGN   Bo – Bo

Built: 1965 – 66 by English Electric Co. at Vulcan Foundry, Newton le Willows or BR at Doncaster Works. Later rebuilt with resilient wheels and flexicoil suspension. Tap changer control.
Traction Motors: AEI 282AZ.
Max. Tractive Effort: 258 kN (58000 lbf).
Continuous Rating: 2680 kW (3600 hp) giving a tractive effort of 89 kN (20000 lbf) at 67 mph.
Maximum Rail Power: 4400 kW (5900 hp) at 38 mph.

Brake Force: 40 t.	**Length over Buffers:** 17.83 m.
Design Speed: 100 m.p.h.	**Weight:** 83 t – 84 t.
Max. Speed: 100 (100*) m.p.h.	**RA:** 6.
ETH Index: 66	**Wheel Diameter:** 1156 mm.
Train Brakes: Air & Vacuum.	**Electric Brake:** Rheostatic.

Class 86/6 have the ETH equipment isolated.

DFNC locos between 86612 and 86639 are owned by Porterbrook Leasing Company. Others are owned by Freightliner 1995 Ltd.
Class 86/4 are owned by English Welsh & Scottish Railway.

86401		RX	PXLE	CE	
86602	a*	F	DFNC	CE	
86603	a*	FD	DFNC	CE	
86604	a*	FF	DFNC	CE	
86605	a*	FD	DFNC	CE	Intercontainer
86606	a*	FF	DFNC	CE	
86607	a*	FD	DFNC	CE	The Institution of Electrical Engineers
86608	a*	FE	DFNC	CE	St. John Ambulance
86609	a*	FD	DFNC	CE	
86610	a*	FD	DFNC	CE	
86611	a*	FD	DFNC	CE	Airey Neave
86612	a*	FF	DFNC	CE	Elizabeth Garrett Anderson
86613	a*	F	DFNC	CE	County of Lancashire
86614	a*	FD	DFNC	CE	Frank Hornby

86615	a*	F	DFNC	CE	Rotary International
86416		RX	PXLE	CE	
86417		RX	PXLE	CE	
86618	a*	FF	DFNC	CE	
86419		RX	PXLE	CE	
86620	a*	F	DFNC	CE	
86621	a*	FD	DFNC	CE	London School of Economics
86622	a*	FE	DFNC	CE	
86623	a*	FF	DFNC	CE	
86424		RX	PXLE	CE	
86425		RX	PXLE	CE	Saint Mungo
86426		RX	PXLE	CE	
86627	a*	F	DFNC	CE	The Industrial Society
86628	a*	FF	DFNC	CE	Aldaniti
86430		RX	PXLE	CE	Saint Edmund
86631	a*	FD	DFNC	CE	
86632	a*	F	DFNC	CE	Brookside
86633	a*	F	DFNC	CE	Wulfruna
86634	a*	F	DFNC	CE	University of London
86635	a*	FD	DFNC	CE	
86636	a*	F	DFNC	CE	
86637	a*	FF	DFNC	CE	
86638	a*	FF	DFNC	CE	
86639	a*	FD	DFNC	CE	

CLASS 87   BR DESIGN   Bo – Bo

Built: 1973 – 75 by BREL at Crewe Works.
Traction Motors: GEC G412AZ frame mounted (87/0), G412BZ (87/1).
Max. Tractive Effort: 258 kN (58000 lbf).
Continuous Rating: 3730 kW (5000 hp) giving a tractive effort of 95 kN (21300 lbf) at 87 mph (Class 87/0), 3620 kW (4850 hp) giving a tractive effort of 96 kN (21600 lbf) at 84 mph (Class 87/1).
Maximum Rail Power: 5860 kW (7860 hp) at 50.8 mph.

Brake Force: 40 t.	**Length over Buffers:** 17.83 m.
Design Speed: 110 mph	**Weight:** 83.5 t.
Max. Speed: 110 (75*) m.p.h.	**RA:** 6.
ETH Index: 95 (75§)	**Wheel Diameter:** 1150 mm.
Train Brakes: Air.	**Electric Brake:** Rheostatic.

Class 87/0. Standard Design. Tap Changer Control.

Owned by Porterbrook Leasing Company.

87001	I	IWCA	WN	Royal Scot
87002	I	IWCA	WN	Royal Sovereign
87003	I	IWCA	WN	Patriot
87004	I	IWCA	WN	Britannia
87005	I	IWCA	WN	City of London
87006	I	IWCA	WN	City of Glasgow
87007	I	IWCA	WN	City of Manchester

87008	I	IWCA	WN	City of Liverpool
87009 §	I	IWCA	WN	City of Birmingham
87010	I	IWCA	WN	King Arthur
87011	I	IWCA	WN	The Black Prince
87012	I	IWCA	WN	The Royal Bank of Scotland
87013	I	IWCA	WN	John O' Gaunt
87014	I	IWCA	WN	Knight of the Thistle
87015	I	IWCA	WN	Howard of Effingham
87016	I	IWCA	WN	Willesden Intercity Depot
87017	I	IWCA	WN	Iron Duke
87018	I	IWCA	WN	Lord Nelson
87019	I	IWCA	WN	Sir Winston Churchill
87020	I	IWCA	WN	North Briton
87021	I	IWCA	WN	Robert the Bruce
87022	I	IWCA	WN	Cock o' the North
87023	I	IWCA	WN	Velocity
87024	I	IWCA	WN	Lord of the Isles
87025	I	IWCA	WN	County of Cheshire
87026	I	IWCA	WN	Sir Richard Arkwright
87027	I	IWCA	WN	Wolf of Badenoch
87028	I	IWCA	WN	Lord President
87029 §	I	IWCA	WN	Earl Marischal
87030	I	IWCA	WN	Black Douglas
87031	I	IWCA	WN	Hal o' the Wynd
87032	I	IWCA	WN	Kenilworth
87033	I	IWCA	WN	Thane of Fife
87034	I	IWCA	WN	William Shakespeare
87035	I	IWCA	WN	Robert Burns

Class 87/1. Thyristor Control.

87101	*	DAMC	CE	STEPHENSON

CLASS 89   BRUSH DESIGN   Co – Co

Built: 1987 by BREL, Crewe Works.
Traction Motors: Brush design (frame mounted).
Max. Tractive Effort: 205 kN (46000 lbf).
Continuous Rating: 2390 kW (3200 hp) giving a tractive effort of 105 kN (23600 lbf) at 92 mph.
Maximum Rail Power:.
Brake Force: 40 t.
Design Speed: 125 m.p.h.
Max. Speed: 125 m.p.h.
ETH Index: 95
Train Brakes: Air.
Couplings: Drop-head buckeye.
Length over Buffers: 18.80 m.
Weight: 104 t.
RA: 6.
Wheel Diameter: 1150 mm.
Electric Brake: Rheostatic.

Owned by Great North Eastern Railway.

89001	I	IECA	BN	Avocet

CLASS 90   GEC DESIGN   Bo–Bo

Built: 1987–90 by BREL at Crewe Works. Thyristor control.
Traction Motors: GEC G412CY separately excited frame mounted.
Max. Tractive Effort: 258 kN (58000 lbf).
Continuous Rating: 3730 kW (5000 hp) giving a tractive effort of 95 kN (21300 lbf) at 87 mph.
Maximum Rail Power: 5860 kW (7860 hp) at 68.3 mph.

Brake Force: 40 t.	**Length over Buffers:** 18.80 m.
Design Speed: 110 m.p.h.	**Weight:** 84.5 t.
Max. Speed: 110 (75*) m.p.h.	**RA:** 7.
ETH Index: 95	**Wheel Diameter:** 1156 mm.
Train Brakes: Air.	**Electric Brake:** Rheostatic.

Couplings: Drop-head buckeye (removed on Class 90/1).

Non-standard Liveries:

90128 is in SNCB/NMBS (Belgian Railways) electric loco livery.
90129 is in DB (German Federal Railways) 'neurot' livery.
90130 is in SNCF (French Railways) 'Sybic' livery.
90136 is in livery 'FE', but with full yellow ends and roof and red 'Railfreight Distribution' lettering.

IWCA and DFLC locos are owned by Porterbrook Leasing Company.
PXLE locos are owned by English Welsh & Scottish Railway.

Class 90/0. As built.

90001	I	IWCA	WN	BBC Midlands Today
90002	I	IWCA	WN	The Girls' Brigade
90003	I	IWCA	WN	THE HERALD
90004	I	IWCA	WN	The D' Oyly Carte Opera Company
90005	I	IWCA	WN	Financial Times
90006	I	IWCA	WN	High Sheriff
90007	I	IWCA	WN	Lord Stamp
90008	I	IWCA	WN	The Birmingham Royal Ballet
90009	I	IWCA	WN	The Economist
90010	I	IWCA	WN	275 Railway Squadron (Volunteers)
90011	I	IWCA	WN	The Chartered Institute of Transport
90012	I	IWCA	WN	British Transport Police
90013	I	IWCA	WN	The Law Society
90014	I	IWCA	WN	'The Liverpool Phil'
90015	I	IWCA	WN	BBC North West
90016	RX	PXLE	CE	
90017	RX	PXLE	CE	Rail express systems Quality Assured
90018	RX	PXLE	CE	
90019	RX	PXLE	CE	Penny Black
90020	RX	PXLE	CE	Colonel Bill Cockburn CBE TD
90021	FE	DAMC	CE	
90022	FE	DAMC	CE	Freightconnection
90023	FE	DAMC	CE	
90024	FE	DAMC	CE	

Class 90/1. ETH equipment isolated.

90125	*	**FE** DAMC	CE	
90126	*	**FE** DAMC	CE	Crewe International
				Electric Maintenance Depot
90127	*	**FD** DAMC	CE	Allerton T&RS Depot Quality Approved
90128	*	**O** DAMC	CE	Vrachtverbinding
90129	*	**O** DAMC	CE	Frachtverbindungen
90130	*	**O** DAMC	CE	Fretconnection
90131	*	**FE** DAMC	CE	
90132	*	**FE** DAMC	CE	Cerestar
90133	*	**FE** DAMC	CE	
90134	*	**FE** DAMC	CE	
90135	*	**FE** DAMC	CE	Crewe Basford Hall
90136	*	**O** DAMC	CE	
90137	*	**F** DAMC	CE	
90138	*	**FE** DAMC	CE	
90139	*	**FD** DAMC	CE	
90140	*	**FD** DAMC	CE	
90141	*	**F** DFLC	CE	
90142	*	**F** DFLC	CE	
90143	*	**FF** DFLC	CE	Freightliner Coatbridge
90144	*	**F** DFLC	CE	
90145	*	**FD** DFLC	CE	
90146	*	**FF** DFLC	CE	
90147	*	**FF** DFLC	CE	
90148	*	**FF** DFLC	CE	
90149	*	**F** DFLC	CE	
90150	*	**FF** DFLC	CE	

CLASS 91   GEC DESIGN   Bo – Bo

Built: 1988 – 91 by BREL at Crewe Works. Thyristor control.
Traction Motors: GEC G426AZ.
Continuous Rating: 4540 kW (6090 hp).
Maximum Rail Power: 4700 kW (6300 hp).

Brake Force: 45 t.	**Length over Buffers:** 19.40 m.
Design Speed: 140 m.p.h.	**Weight:** 84 t.
Max. Speed: 140 m.p.h.	**RA:** 7.
ETH Index: 95	**Wheel Diameter:** 1000 mm.
Train Brakes: Air.	**Electric Brake:** Rheostatic.
Couplings: Drop-head buckeye.	

This class is owned by Eversholt Train Leasing Company.

91001	**I**	IECA	BN	Swallow
91002	**I**	IECA	BN	Durham Cathedral
91003	**I**	IECA	BN	THE SCOTSMAN
91004	**I**	IECA	BN	The Red Arrows
91005	**I**	IECA	BN	Royal Air Force Regiment
91006	**GN**	IECA	BN	
91007	**GN**	IECA	BN	

91008	I	IECA	BN	Thomas Cook
91009	I	IECA	BN	Saint Nicholas
91010	I	IECA	BN	Northern Rock
91011	I	IECA	BN	Terence Cuneo
91012	I	IECA	BN	
91013	I	IECA	BN	Michael Faraday
91014	I	IECA	BN	Northern Electric
91015	I	IECA	BN	
91016	I	IECA	BN	
91017	GN	IECA	BN	
91018	I	IECA	BN	Robert Louis Stevenson
91019	GN	IECA	BN	Scottish Enterprise
91020	I	IECA	BN	
91021	I	IECA	BN	Royal Armouries
91022	I	IECA	BN	Robert Adley
91023	I	IECA	BN	
91024	I	IECA	BN	Reverend W Awdry
91025	GN	IECA	BN	
91026	I	IECA	BN	Voice of the North
91027	I	IECA	BN	Great North Run
91028	I	IECA	BN	Guide Dog
91029	I	IECA	BN	Queen Elizabeth II
91030	I	IECA	BN	Palace of Holyroodhouse
91031	I	IECA	BN	Sir Henry Royce

CLASS 92   BRUSH DESIGN   Co – Co

Built: 1993 – 5 by Brush Traction at Loughborough. Thyristor control.
Supply System: 25 kV a.c. from overhead equipment and 750 V d.c. third rail.
Electrical equipment: ABB Transportation, Zürich, Switzerland.
Traction Motors: Brush.
Max. Tractive Effort: 400 kN (90 000 lbf).
Continuous Rating at Motor Shaft: 5040 kW (6760 hp).
Maximum Rail Power (25 kV a.c.): 5000 kW (6700 hp).
Maximum Rail Power (750 V d.c.): 4000 kW (5360 hp).

Brake Force: t.	**Length over Buffers:** 21.34 m.
Design Speed: 140 km/h.	**Weight:** 126 t.
Max. Speed: 140 km/h (87.5 m.p.h.).	**RA:** 8.
ETH Index: 108.	**Wheel Diameter:** 1160 mm.

Train Brakes: Air.
Electric Brake: Rheostatic & regenerative.
Multiple Working: Time division multiplex system.
Communication Equipment: Driver – guard telephone and cab to shore radio-telephone.
Cab Signalling: Fitted with TVM430 cab signalling for Channel Tunnel.

Note: Locos are in Railfreight Distribution ownwership (RfD) except where stated as f – SNCF or p – Eurostar (GB) Ltd. Railfreight Distribution, Eurostar or SNCF logos are being applied.

92001	E	DADC	CE	Victor Hugo
92002	E	DADC	CE	H G Wells
92003	E	DAEC	CE	Beethoven
92004	E	DADC	CE	Jane Austen
92005	E	DAVC	CE	Mozart
92006 f	E	DAVC	CE	Louis Armand
92007	E	DAVC	CE	Schubert
92008	E	DAVC	CE	Jules Verne
92009	E	DAVC	CE	Elgar
92010 f	E	DADC	CE	Molière
92011	E	DADC	CE	Handel
92012	E	DADC	CE	Thomas Hardy
92013	E	DAEC	CE	Puccini
92014 f	E	DAVC	CE	Emile Zola
92015	E	DADC	CE	D H Lawrence
92016	E	DAEC	CE	Brahms
92017	E	DAVC	CE	Shakespeare
92018 f	E	DAEC	CE	Stendhal
92019	E	DAEC	CE	Wagner
92020 p	E	DADC	CE	Milton
92021 p	E	DAVC	CE	Purcell
92022	E	DAVC	CE	Charles Dickens
92023 f	E	DAEC	CE	Ravel
92024	E	DAEC	CE	J S Bach
92025	E	DAEC	CE	Oscar Wilde
92026	E	DAEC	CE	Britten
92027	E	DAEC	CE	George Eliot
92028 f	E	DADC	CE	Saint Saëns
92029	E	DAEC	CE	Dante
92030	E	DADC	CE	De Falla
92031	E	DAEC	CE	
92032 p	E	DAEC	CE	César Franck
92033 f	E	DAVC	CE	Berlioz
92034	E	DAVC	CE	Kipling
92035	E	DAVC	CE	Mendelssohn
92036	E	DAVC	CE	Bertolt Brecht
92037	E	DADC	CE	Sullivan
92038 f	E	DAEC	CE	Voltaire
92039	E	DADC	CE	Johann Strauss
92040 p	E	DAVC	CE	Goethe
92041	E	DAVC	CE	Vaughan Williams
92042	E	DAVC	CE	Ashford
92043 f	E	DAVC	CE	Debussy
92044 p	E	DAVC	CE	Couperin
92045 p	E	DAVC	CE	Chaucer
92046 p	E	DAVC	CE	Sweelinck

3. SERVICE LOCOMOTIVES

CLASS 97/6   RUSTON SHUNTER   0-6-0

Built: 1959 by Ruston & Hornsby at Lincoln.
Engine: Ruston 6VPH of 123 kW (165 hp).
Main Generator: British Thomson Houston RTB6034.
Traction Motor: One British Thomson Houston RTA5041.
Max. Tractive Effort: 75 kN (17000 lbf).

Brake Force: 16 t.		**Length over Buffers:** 7.62 m.	
Weight: 31 t.		**Wheel Diameter:** 978 mm.	
Max. Speed: 20 mph.		**RA:** 1.	

Non-Standard Livery: Civil Engineer's Yellow.

97651	(PWM 651)	v	**0** RNRG	RG (U)
97654	(PWM 654)	v	**0** RNRG	RG

CLASS 97/8   EE SHUNTER   0-6-0

For details see Class 09. Severn Tunnel emergency train locomotive.

Non-Standard Livery: BR blue with grey cab.

97806	(09017)	x	**0** LNCF	CF	Normally kept at Sudbrook.

4. LOCOMOTIVES AWAITING DISPOSAL

03079	Sandown IoW
03179 **N**	Ryde T&RSMD
08222	Bounds Green T&RSMD
08390	ADtranz Crewe Works
08419	ADtranz Crewe Works
08473	Leicester LIP
08515	Gateshead WRD
08562	Stratford TMD
08565	Motherwell TMD
08609	Willesden TMD
08618	Gateshead WRD
08634	Stratford TMD
08666	Allerton TMD
08673 **IO**	Allerton TMD
08677	Willesden TMD
08707	ADtranz Crewe Works
08733	Motherwell TMD
08755	Millerhill FP
08760	Wessex Traincare
08793 **O**	Aberdeen Guild St. Yard
08829	Toton TMD
08849	ADtranz Crewe Works
08855	Aberdeen Guild St. Yard
08880	Allerton TMD
08895	Margam WRD
08898	Bescot TMD
20073	Bescot Yard
20119	Toton TMD
20154	Toton TMD
20177	Toton TMD
25083	Crewe Carriage Shed
31168	Bescot Yard
31180 **FR**	Toton Yard
31184 **FO**	Toton Yard
31196 **C**	Stratford TMD
31209 **FA**	Toton Yard
31217 **FC**	Toton Yard
31282 **FR**	Bescot Yard
31283 **O**	Stratford TMD
31286	Bescot Yard
31289	Bescot Yard
31290 **C**	Toton Yard
31296 **FA**	Crewe Carriage Shed
31299 **FO**	Stratford TMD
31320	Stratford TMD
31402	Bescot Yard
31403	Toton Yard

31428	Bescot Yard
31442	Crewe Carriage Shed
31460	Bescot Yard
31547 **C**	Toton Yard
31553 **C**	Toton Yard
31569 **C**	Toton Yard
31970	ADtranz Crewe Works
33020	Stewarts Lane T&RSMD
33021 **FM**	Eastleigh T&RSMD
33033 **FA**	Stewarts Lane T&RSMD
33035 **N**	Eastleigh T&RSMD
33038	Stratford TMD
33040	Stewarts Lane T&RSMD
33042 **FA**	Stewarts Lane T&RSMD
33047 **C**	Eastleigh Yard
33050 **FA**	Stewarts Lane T&RSMD
33064 **FA**	Old Oak Common TMD
33101 **D**	Eastleigh T&RSMD
33108 **C**	Eastleigh T&RSMD
33113	Stewarts Lane T&RSMD
33118 **C**	Eastleigh T&RSMD
33201 **C**	Stewarts Lane T&RSMD
33206 **FD**	Eastleigh T&RSMD
33211 **FD**	Stewarts Lane T&RSMD
37031 **FD**	Cardiff Canton T&RSMD
37080 **FP**	Cardiff Canton T&RSMD
37252 **FD**	Doncaster TMD
37280 **FP**	Old Oak Common TMD
37373 **FR**	Old Oak Common TMD
45015	Toton TMD
47063 **FA**	ADtranz Crewe Works
47096	Tinsley TMD
47102	Tinsley TMD
47108	Old Oak Common TMD
47112 **FO**	Old Oak Common TMD
47121	Old Oak Common TMD
47190 **FP**	Tinsley TMD
47214 **FD**	Tinsley TMD
47249 **FR**	Tinsley TMD
47318 **FO**	Bescot Yard
47320 **FO**	ADtranz Crewe Works
47321 **F**	Tinsley TMD
47325 **FO**	Tinsley TMD
47421	ADtranz Crewe Works
47423	Old Oak Common TMD
47425	Old Oak Common TMD
47426 **BR**	Old Oak Common TMD

47430	**FA**	Old Oak Common TMD	47515	**M**	Crewe Coal Siding
47431	**BR**	Old Oak Common TMD	47538	**BR**	ADtranz Crewe Works
47438	**BR**	Old Oak Common TMD	47707	**RX**	Crewe TMD (D)
47439	**BR**	ADtranz Crewe Works	47714	**RX**	Crewe TMD (D)
47440	**BR**	Old Oak Common TMD	47850	**I**	ADtranz Crewe Works
47441	**BR**	Old Oak Common TMD	47973	**M**	ADtranz Crewe Works
47442	**BR**	ADtranz Crewe Works	56013	**FC**	Toton TMD
47443	**BR**	ADtranz Crewe Works	56016	**FC**	Cardiff Canton T&RSMD
47446	**BR**	Old Oak Common TMD	56023	**FC**	Toton TMD
47452	**BR**	Old Oak Common TMD	56028	**FC**	Margam WRD
47453	**BR**	Old Oak Common TMD	56030	**FC**	Margam WRD
47457	**BR**	Old Oak Common TMD	56122	**FC**	Toton TMD
47463		ADtranz Crewe Works	73003	**G**	Old Oak Common TMD
47465	**BR**	Old Oak Common TMD	73111	**I0**	Stewarts Lane T&RSMD
47466	**BR**	ADtranz Crewe Works	86239	**RX**	Crewe Int. TMD (E)
47472		Old Oak Common TMD	97653	**0**	Reading T&RSMD
47485	**BR**	ADtranz Crewe Works			

Non-Standard Liveries:

08793 is in London & North Eastern Railway apple green.
31283 is BR blue with large numbers.
31970 is BR Research light grey, dark grey, white and red.
97653 is Departmental yellow.

▲ Class 56 No. 56089 is pictured on the Felixstowe branch at Levington on 10th July 1996. The train is a special Crewe–Felixstowe Freightliner service. *John A. Day*

▼ Two-tone grey with Mainline branding is the livery carried by Class 58 No. 58035 in this view of the loco taken at Stratford. The date is 17th August 1996. *Kevin Conkey*

Foster Yeoman Class 59 No. 59005 'KENNETH J. PAINTER' approaches West Ealing from the east with an empty stone train on 28th July 1995.

Ian A. Lyall

Loadhaul liveried Class 60 No. 60007 passes Gateforth with a Leeds to Lindsey tank train on 20th May, 1996.

Ian A. Lyall

The 11.12 Jarrow–Stanlow empty tank train is pictured passing Cowperthwaite, north of Oxenholme behind Transrail liveried Class 60 No. 60056 'William Beveridge'. The date is 17th July 1996.

Nic Joynson

▲ Freshly repainted in English, Welsh & Scottish Railway (EW&S) livery, Class 73 No. 73128 is pictured stabled at Eastleigh T&RSMD on 24th September 1996. *Brian Denton*

▼ InterCity liveried Class 86 No. 86229 'Sir John Betjeman' passes Mealbank with the Glasgow Central–Brighton 'Sussex Scot' service on 26th May 1995. *Dave McAlone*

A Euston bound train is seen passing the site of the Keswick branch at Penrith on 5th August 1995 behind Class 87 No. 87029 'Earl Marischal'.

Dave McAlone

▲ Rail express systems liveried Class 90 No. 90019 'Penny Black' passes Hambleton South Junction with the 14.50 Low Fell–London Kings Cross mail train on 12th July 1995. *Hugh Ballantyne*

▼ Class 91 No. 91019 'Scottish Enterprise' is pictured at Esholt whilst working the 11.38 Bradford Forster Square–London Kings Cross service on 21st October 1996. Both the loco and the coaching stock are carrying the new Great North Eastern Railway livery *Les Nixon*

Class 92s are now starting to enter traffic. Here, Class 92 No. 92010 'Molière' passes Otford Junction with the 09.37 Wembley–Dollands Moor service on 1st October 1996. The loco carries European Passenger Services livery.

Rodney Lissenden

POOL CODES & ALLOCATIONS

CENTRAL SERVICES

CDJD Derby Etches Park Class 08 (Research)

08417　08956

RAILFREIGHT DISTRIBUTION

DAAN Allerton Class 08

08569	08653 **FE**	08703	08739	08784	08799	08825
08837 **D**	08842	08856	08872 **D**	08907 **0**	08939	08951 **D**

DADC Crewe Electric Class 92 (Dollands Moor-Wembley)

92001 **E**　92002 **E**　92004 **E**　92010 **E**　92011 **E**　92012 **E**　92015 **E**
92020 **E**　92028 **E**　92030 **E**　92037 **E**　92039 **E**

DAEC Crewe Electric Class 92 (Not in Traffic)

92003 **E**　92013 **E**　92016 **E**　92018 **E**　92019 **E**　92023 **E**　92024 **E**
92025 **E**　92026 **E**　92027 **E**　92029 **E**　92031 **E**　92032 **E**　92038 **E**

DAET Tinsley Class 47

47033 **FE** 47049 **FE** 47051 **FE** 47053 **FE** 47085 **FE** 47095 **FE** 47125 **FE**
47145 **0** 47146 **FE** 47150 **FE** 47186 **FE** 47188 **FE** 47194 **FD** 47200 **FE**
47201 **FE** 47210 **FD** 47211 **FD** 47213 **FD** 47217 **FE** 47218 **FE** 47219 **FE**
47226 **FD** 47228 **FE** 47229 **FE** 47237 **FE** 47241 **FE** 47245 **FE** 47258 **FE**
47276 **FE** 47280 **FD** 47281 **FD** 47285 **FD** 47286 **FE** 47287 **FE** 47293 **FE**
47297 **FE** 47298 **FD** 47299 **FD** 47304 **FD** 47306 **FE** 47307 **FE** 47310 **FE**
47312 **FE** 47313 **FD** 47314 **FE** 47316 **FE** 47326 **FE** 47328 **FE** 47330 **FD**
47335 **FD** 47338 **FE** 47344 **FE** 47348 **FE** 47351 **FE** 47355 **FD** 47360 **FE**
47362 **FD** 47363 **F** 47365 **FE** 47375 **FE** 47378 **FD** 47379 **F** 47525 **FE**
47540 **C**

DAMC Crewe Electric Class 87/1 & 90

87101　90021 **FE** 90022 **FE** 90023 **FE** 90024 **FE** 90125 **FE** 90126 **FE**
90127 **FD** 90128 **0** 90129 **0** 90130 **0** 90131 **FE** 90132 **FE** 90133 **FE**
90134 **FE** 90135 **FE** 90136 **0** 90137 **F** 90138 **FE** 90139 **FD** 90140 **FD**

DASY Tinsley Class 08 (Saltley)

08413 **D** 08535 **D** 08694　08751 **FE** 08905 **FE** 08946 **FE**

DATI Tinsley Class 08

08879 **0**

DAVC Crewe Electric Class 92 (100 mph Maximum)

92005 **E**　92006 **E**　92007 **E**　92008 **E**　92009 **E**　92014 **E**　92017 **E**
92021 **E**　92022 **E**　92033 **E**　92034 **E**　92035 **E**　92036 **E**　92040 **E**
92041 **E**　92042 **E**　92043 **E**　92044 **E**　92045 **E**　92046 **E**

DAWE Allerton Class 08/09 (Wembley/Dagenham/Southampton)

08389   08393 **D** 08482 **D** 08655 **F** 08737 **FE** 08844   08913 **D**
09011 **D** 09021 **FE**

DAXT Tinsley Class 47 (Awaiting Repair)

47144 **FD** 47236 **FE** 47284 **FD** 47309 **FD**

DAYX Stored Locomotives

08661 **FE** 08902   08926   09022   47222 **FD** 47291 **FD** 47555 **FE**

FREIGHTLINER 1995

DFLC Crewe Electric Class 90/1

90141 **F** 90142 **F** 90143 **FF** 90144 **F** 90145 **FD** 90146 **FF** 90147 **FF**
90148 **FF** 90149 **F** 90150 **FF**

DFLM Crewe Diesel Class 47 (Multiple Working Fitted)

47114 **FD** 47152 **FF** 47204 **F** 47205 **FF** 47209 **FF** 47234 **FE** 47290 **FE**
47292 **FD** 47303 **FE** 47323 **FE** 47337 **FF** 47361 **FF**

DFLS Allerton/Crewe Diesel/Eastleigh/Stratford/Tinsley Class 08

08530 **D** 08531 **D** 08575 **BS** 08585   08624   08642 **O** 08691 **G**
08745 **FE** 08891   08892 **D**

DFLT Crewe Diesel Class 47

47052 **FF** 47060 **F** 47147 **F** 47157 **FF** 47197 **F** 47206 **FF** 47212 **F**
47225 **FF** 47231 **F** 47270 **FF** 47283 **F** 47289 **F** 47296 **FF** 47301 **FF**
47302 **FR** 47305 **FF** 47317 **F** 47339 **F** 47345 **FF** 47347 **F** 47349 **F**
47350 **FO** 47354 **FF** 47358 **FF** 47370 **FE** 47371 **FF** 47376 **FF** 47377 **F**

DFNC Crewe Electric Class 86/6

86602 **F** 86603 **FD** 86604 **FF** 86605 **FD** 86606 **FF** 86607 **FD** 86608 **FE**
86609 **FD** 86610 **FD** 86611 **FD** 86612 **FF** 86613 **F** 86614 **FD** 86615 **F**
86618 **FF** 86620 **F** 86621 **FF** 86622 **FF** 86623 **F** 86627 **F** 86628 **FF**
86631 **FD** 86632 **F** 86633 **F** 86634 **F** 86635 **FD** 86636 **F** 86637 **FF**
86638 **FF** 86639 **FD**

DHLT Crewe Diesel Class 47 (Holding Pool)

47019 **FO** 47079 **FE** 47142 **FR** 47156 **FD** 47187 **F** 47207 **F** 47279 **FF**
47322 **FR** 47340 **C** 47356 **FO** 47367 **FR** 47473 **BR**

EW&S (FORMERLY MAINLINE)

ENAN Toton/Stewarts Lane Class 60

60001 **FA** 60006 **FM** 60009 **FM** 60010 **FM** 60011 **ML** 60012 **EW** 60017 **EW**
60018 **FM** 60019 **EW** 60039 **FM** 60040 **EW** 60041 **FM** 60042 **FM** 60043 **FM**
60044 **ML** 60048 **EW** 60071 **FM** 60072 **FM** 60073 **FM** 60074 **FM** 60075 **FM**
60076 **FM** 60077 **FM** 60078 **ML** 60079 **FM** 60083 **FM** 60086 **FM** 60087 **FM**
60088 **FM** 60094 **FM** 60098 **FM** 60099 **FM** 60100 **FM**

ENBN   Toton Class 58

58001	FM	58002	ML	58003	FM	58004	FM	58005	ML
58006	F	58007	FM						
58008	ML	58009	FM	58010	FM	58011	FM	58012	FM
58013	ML	58014	ML						
58015	FM	58016	EW	58017	FM	58018	FM	58019	FM
58020	FM	58021	ML						
58022	FM	58023	ML	58024	EW	58025	FM	58026	FM
58027	FM	58028	FM						
58029	FM	58030	FM	58031	FM	58032	ML	58033	EW
58034	FM	58035	FM						
58036	ML	58037	FM	58038	FM	58039	FM	58040	FM
58041	FM	58042	ML						
58043	FM	58044	FM	58045	FM	58046	ML	58047	FM
58048	EW	58049	EW						
58050	ML								

ENRN   Toton Class 47 (Restricted Use)

47004 **G** 47016 **FO** 47315 **C** 47702 **F**

ENSN   Toton Class 08/09 (Toton/Peterborough)

08441		08492		08495		08511		08528	D
08529		08538	D						
08580		08886	EW	09201	D				

ENTN   Toton Class 31/37 (Infrastructure)

31407	ML	31466	C	37010	C	37012	C	37013	ML
37038	C	37042	EW						
37046	C	37051	EW	37055	ML	37057	EW	37065	ML
37072	D	37079	FD						
37097	C	37098	C	37114	EW	37137	FM	37162	D
37185	C	37222	FM						
37227	FM	37238	F	37244	F	37248	ML	37264	C
37376	FC	37715	FM						
37798	ML								

ENXX   Stored Locomotives

08449		08607		08723		08773		31116	O
31135	C	31149	FR						
31165	G	31181	C	31186	C	31187	C	31191	C
31205	FR	31219	C						
31230	FO	31247	FR	31250	C	31252	FO	31268	C
31271	FA	31276	FC						
31294	FA	31308	C	31531	C	31541	C	31549	C
31551	C	31552	C						
31558	C	31459		31461	D	31563	C	33002	C
33008	G	33012							
33023		33029		33048		33052		33053	FA
33057	C	33063	FM						
33065	FM	33103	C	33117		33204	FM	33207	FM
37035	C	37048	FM						
37092	C	37241	F	37278	FC	47223	F	47278	FP
47366	C	47368	F						
47462	R	47484	G	47526	BR	47711	N	47802	I
47803	O	73126	N						

ENZX   Locomotives for Withdrawal

08540 **D** 08597 33205 **FD**

EWDB   Stewarts Lane/Stratford Class 33/37 (Infrastructure)

33019	C	33025	C	33026	C	33030	C	33046	C
33051	C	33109	D						
33116		33202	C	33208	C	37023	ML	37037	FM
37047	ML	37054	C						
37074	ML	37077	ML	37106	C	37109	EW	37140	C
37167	C	37198	ML						
37203	ML	37216	ML	37219	ML	37242	ML	37274	ML
37371	ML	37375	ML						
37377	C	37379	ML	37667	F	37676	F	37678	FM
37679	F	37703	FM						
37705	FM	37709	FM	37800	FM	37803	ML	37890	FM
37891	FM	37892	FM						

EWEB   Stewarts Lane Class 73 (Infrastructure)

73101	EW	73103	IO	73104	IO	73105	C	73106	D
73107	C	73108	C						
73110	C	73114	ML	73117	IO	73119	C	73129	N
73133	ML	73134	IO						
73136	ML	73138	C						

EWEH   **Eastleigh Class 08**

08854   08940

EWHG   **Stewarts Lane Class 09**

09003   09009 **EW** 09019 **ML** 09024 **ML**

EWOC   **Old Oak Common Class 08/09**

08480 **G** 08523 **ML** 08526   08646 **F** 08651 **D** 08664   08709
08904   08924 **D** 08944 **D** 08947   09006 **ML** 09007 **ML** 09012 **D**
09016 **D** 09018 **ML** 09101 **D** 09102 **D**

EWRB   **Stewarts Lane Class 37/73 (Restricted Use)**

37040 **EW** 37174 **C** 37194 **FM** 37220 **EW** 37245 **C** 37293 **ML** 37370 **EW**
37372 **ML** 37380 **FM** 73128 **EW** 73131 **EW** 73132 **IO** 73139 **IO** 73140 **IO**
73141 **IO**

EWSF   **Stratford Class 08/09**

08541 **D** 08593 **O** 08750   08752 **C** 08775   08866   08909
09010 **D** 09020

EWSU   **Selhurst Class 08/09**

08698   09023

EWSX   **Stored/Reserve Shunters**

08414 **O** 08460 **O** 08517   08542 **F** 08600 **D** 08670   08689 **O**
08700   08715 **O** 08740 **F** 08758   08811   08828   08878
08933 **EW** 08957   08958

EW&S (FORMERLY LOADHAUL)

FDAI   **Immingham Class 60**

60002 **FP** 60003 **FP** 60007 **LH** 60013 **FP** 60014 **EW** 60021 **FS** 60022 **U**
60024 **EW** 60025 **LH** 60026 **EW** 60027 **EW** 60028 **FP** 60038 **LH** 60051 **FP**
60054 **FP** 60059 **LH** 60064 **FL** 60067 **F** 60070 **FL** 60090 **FC** 60091 **FC**

FDBI   **Immingham Class 56 (Humberside)**

56021 **LH** 56041 **U** 56055 **LH** 56068 **U** 56077 **LH** 56089 **EW** 56090 **LH**
56100 **LH** 56102 **LH** 56106 **LH** 56107 **LH** 56109 **LH** 56111 **LH** 56116 **LH**
56118 **LH** 56120 **EW**

FDBK   **Immingham Class 56 (Aire Valley)**

56027 **LH** 56034 **LH** 56038 **FT** 56043 **LH** 56051 **EW** 56067 **EW** 56075 **F**
56078 **F** 56080 **F** 56082 **F** 56083 **LH** 56085 **LH** 56087 **FS** 56088 **EW**
56091 **F** 56094 **FC** 56126 **FC** 56131 **F** 56135 **F**

FDCI   Immingham Class 37

37513 **LH** 37515 **LH** 37516 **LH** 37517 **EW** 37519 **FS** 37677 **F** 37680 **FA**
37682 **EW** 37684 **EW** 37686 **FA** 37688 **EW** 37689 **F** 37694 **FC** 37697 **EW**
37698 **LH** 37706 **EW** 37707 **EW** 37708 **FP** 37710 **LH** 37711 **FS** 37713 **LH**
37716 **FS** 37717 **EW** 37718 **EW** 37719 **FP** 37883 **EW** 37884 **LH** 37885 **U**
37886 **EW** 37888 **F**

FDKI   Immingham Class 47 (Control Contingency)

47224 **FP** 47331 **C** 47476 **R** 47543 **R** 47574 **R** 47981 **C**

FDRI   Immingham Class 37 (Restricted Use)

37131 **F** 37225 **F** 37332 **FC** 37350 **FP** 37358 **F** 37503 **EW**

FDSD   Doncaster Class 08

08418 **F** 08500 **O** 08509 **F** 08510   08512 **F** 08514   08587
08877 **D**

FDSI   Immingham Class 08

08401 **D** 08405 **D** 08632   08665   08824 **F** 08888 **EW**

FDSK   Knottingley Class 08/09

08442 **F** 08499 **F** 08516 **D** 08605   08662   08706   08776 **D**
08782   08783   09014 **D**

FDSX   Stored Shunters

08388 **FP** 08445   08466 **FO** 08581 **BS** 08713   08903   08931

FDYX   Stored Locomotives

37003 **C** 37019 **FD** 37045 **F** 37058 **C** 37059 **FD** 37063 **FD** 37068 **FD**
37075 **F** 37083 **C** 37104 **C** 37110 **F** 37139 **FC** 37144 **FA** 37209 **BR**
37217   37218 **F** 37223 **FC** 37235 **F** 37298 **F** 37331 **F** 37333 **FD**
37335 **F** 37340 **FD** 37341 **F** 37343 **C** 37344 **FD** 37345 **FD** 37359 **FP**
37381 **FD** 37382 **FP** 37699 **FC** 47221 **FP** 47256 **FD** 47277 **FD** 47294 **FD**
47319 **FP** 47346 **C** 47352 **C** 47359 **FD** 47369 **FD** 47550 **M** 47676 **I**
47677 **I** 56008   56011 **F** 56012 **FC** 56014 **FC**

FMAY   Thornaby Class 60

60004 **EW** 60008 **LH** 60020 **FS** 60023 **FS** 60030 **FS** 60031 **FS** 60049 **FS**
60050 **EW** 60052 **FS** 60053 **FP** 60068 **F** 60069 **F**

FMBY   Thornaby Class 56

56003 **LH** 56006 **LH** 56031 **C** 56035 **LH** 56039 **LH** 56045 **LH** 56046 **C**
56048 **C** 56050 **LH** 56061 **FS** 56062 **F** 56063 **F** 56065 **FA** 56069 **FS**
56074 **LH** 56081 **F** 56084 **LH** 56095 **F** 56097 **FS** 56098 **F** 56108 **F**
56110 **LH** 56112 **LH** 56117 **FC** 56130 **LH** 56134 **FC**

FMSY   Thornaby Class 08/09

08577   08582 **D** 08806 **F** 08813 **D** 09005 **D** 09106 **D** 09204 **D**

EUROPEAN PASSENGER SERVICES

GPSN   Stewarts Lane Class 73 (North Pole)

73118 **E**   73130 **E**

GPSS   Old Oak Common Class 08 (North Pole)

08948 **E**

GPSV   Old Oak Common Class 37/6

37601 **E**   37602 **E**   37603 **E**   37604 **E**   37605 **E**   37606 **E**   37607 **E**
37608 **E**   37609 **E**   37610 **E**   37611 **E**   37612 **E**

TRAIN OPERATING UNITS

HASS   ScotRail - Inverness Class 08

08754   08762

HBSH   Great North Eastern Railway - Bounds Green/Edinburgh Craigentinny
          Class 08

08472   08571   08724   08834 **FD** 08853

HEBD   Merseyrail - Birkenhead North Class 73

73002 **BR** 73005 **O**   73901 **MD** 73906 **MD**

HFSL   West Coast - Longsight Class 08

08611   08721 **O** 08790

HFSN   West Coast - Willesden Class 08

08451   08454   08617   08696 **D** 08887   08934

HGSS   Central - Tyseley Class 08

08616 **G** 08805 **O**

HISE   Midland Mainline - Derby Etches Park Class 08

08536   08690   08697   08899

HISL   Midland Mainline - Neville Hill Class 08

08525 **F** 08588 **BS** 08908   08950 **I**

HJSE   Great Western Trains- Landore Class 08

08780   08795 **M** 08822 **M**

HJSL   Great Western Trains - Laira Class 08

08641 **D** 08644 **I** 08645 **D** 08648 **D** 08663 **D**

HJXX   Great Western Trains - Old Oak Common/St Phillips Marsh Class 08

08410 **D** 08483 **D** 08643 **D** 08836 **I**

HLSV   Cardiff Railway Co. - Cardiff Canton Class 08

08830

HSSN Anglia - Norwich Crown Point Class 08

08810 08869 **G** 08928 **FR**

HWSU Connex South Central - Selhurst Class 09

09004 09025 09026 **D**

HYSB Stagecoach (South Western Trains)- Bournemouth Class 73/1

73109 **N**

INTERCITY TRAIN OPERATING UNITS

IANA Anglia Railways - Norwich Crown Point Class 86/2

86204 I 86215 I 86217 I 86218 I 86220 I 86221 I 86223 I
86228 I 86230 I 86232 I 86235 I 86237 I 86238 I 86246 I
86250 I 86257 I

ICCA CrossCountry Trains - Longsight Class 86/2

86205 I 86206 I 86212 I 86214 I 86216 I 86222 I 86226 I
86227 I 86229 I 86233 I 86234 I 86244 I 86247 I 86252 I
86255 I 86259 I 86260 I

ICCP CrossCountry Trains - Laira Class 43

43006 I 43007 I 43008 I 43091 I 43101 I 43102 I 43103 I
43121 I 43122 I 43153 I 43154 I 43155 I 43156 I 43157 I
43158 I 43159 I 43160 I 43161 I 43162 I 43178 I 43184 I
43193 I 43194 I 43195 I 43196 I 43197 I 43198 I

ICCS CrossCountry Trains - Edinburgh Craigentinny Class 43

43013 I 43014 I 43062 I 43063 I 43065 I 43067 I 43068 I
43069 I 43070 I 43071 I 43078 I 43079 I 43080 I 43084 I
43086 I 43087 I 43088 I 43089 I 43090 I 43092 I 43093 I
43094 I 43097 I 43098 I 43099 I 43100 I 43123 I

IECA Great North Eastern Railway - Bounds Green Class 91

91001 I 91002 I 91003 I 91004 I 91005 I 91006 **GN** 91007 **GN**
91008 I 91009 I 91010 I 91011 I 91012 I 91013 I 91014 I
91015 I 91016 I 91017 **GN** 91018 I 91019 **GN** 91020 I 91021 I
91022 I 91023 I 91024 I 91025 **GN** 91026 I 91027 I 91028 I
91029 I 91030 I 91031 I

IECP Great North Eastern Railway - Craigentinny/Neville Hill Class 43

43038 I 43039 I 43095 I 43096 I 43104 I 43105 I 43106 I
43107 I 43108 I 43109 I 43110 I 43111 I 43112 I 43113 I
43114 I 43115 I 43116 I 43117 **GN** 43118 **GN** 43119 I 43120 **GN**
43167 I

ILRA CrossCountry Trains - Crewe Diesel Class 47/4

47805 I 47806 I 47810 I 47812 I 47814 I 47818 I **47822 I**
47825 I 47826 I 47827 I 47828 I 47829 I 47831 I **47838 I**
47840 I 47841 I 47843 I 47844 I 47847 I 47848 I **47849 I**
47851 I 47853 I 47854 I

ILRB   CrossCountry Trains - Crewe Diesel Class 47/4 (Spot hire)

47807 **PL** 47817 **PL**

IMLP   Midland Mainline - Neville Hill Class 43

43043 I	43044 I	43045 I	43046 I	43047 I	43048 I	43049 I
43050 I	43051 I	43052 I	43053 I	43054 I	43055 I	43056 I
43057 I	43058 I	43059 I	43060 I	43061 I	43064 I	43066 I
43072 I	43073 I	43074 I	43075 I	43076 I	43077 I	43081 I
43082 I	43083 I	43085 I	43180 I			

IVGA   Gatwick Express - Stewarts Lane Class 73

73201 **GE**	73202 **GE**	73203 **GE**	73204 **GE**	73205 **GE**	73206 **GE**	73207 **GE**
73208 **GE**	73209 **GE**	73210 **GE**	73211 **GE**	73212 **GE**	73213 **GE**	73235 **GE**

IWCA   Intercity West Coast - Willesden Class 87/90

87001 I	87002 I	87003 I	87004 I	87005 I	87006 I	87007 I
87008 I	87009 I	87010 I	87011 I	87012 I	87013 I	87014 I
87015 I	87016 I	87017 I	87018 I	87019 I	87020 I	87021 I
87022 I	87023 I	87024 I	87025 I	87026 I	87027 I	87028 I
87029 I	87030 I	87031 I	87032 I	87033 I	87034 I	87035 I
90001 I	90002 I	90003 I	90004 I	90005 I	90006 I	90007 I
90008 I	90009 I	90010 I	90011 I	90012 I	90013 I	90014 I
90015 I						

IWCP   Intercity West Coast - Manchester Longsight Class 43

43028 I	43029 I	43041 I	43042 I	43164 I	43165 I	43166 I

IWLA   Great Western Trains - Laira Class 47

47815 I	47816 I	47832 I	47846 **U**

IWLX   Great Western Trains - Laira Class 47 (Reserve)

47811 I	47813 I	47830 I	47845 I

IWPA   Intercity West Coast - Willesden Class 86

86101 I	86102 I	86207 I	86209 I	86224 I	86225 I	86231 I
86236 I	86240 I	86242 I	86245 I	86248 I	86251 I	86253 I
86256 I	86258 I					

IWRP   Great Western Trains - Laira/St Phillips Marsh Class 43

43002 I	43003 I	43004 I	43005 I	43009 I	43010 I	43011 I
43012 I	43015 **GW**	43016 I	43017 I	43018 I	43019 I	43020 I
43021 I	43022 I	43023 I	43024 I	43025 I	43026 I	43027 I
43030 I	43031 I	43032 I	43033 I	43034 I	43035 I	43036 I
43037 I	43040 I	43124 I	43125 I	43126 I	43127 I	43128 I
43129 **GW**	43130 I	43131 I	43132 I	43133 I	43134 I	43135 **GW**
43136 I	43137 I	43138 I	43139 **GW**	43140 I	43141 I	43142 I
43143 I	43144 I	43145 I	43146 I	43147 I	43148 I	43149 I
43150 I	43151 I	43152 I	43163 I	43168 **GW**	43169 I	43170 I
43171 I	43172 I	43173 I	43174 I	43175 I	43176 I	43177 I
43179 I	43181 I	43182 I	43183 **GW**	43185 **GW**	43186 I	43187 I
43188 I	43189 I	43190 I	43191 **GW**	43192 I		

EW&S (FORMERLY TRANSRAIL)

LBBS   Bescot Class 08/09

08543	D	08567		08601	0	08623		08625		08628		08683	
08746	D	08765	D	08807	BS	08914		08920	F	08927		09104	D

LBDB   Bescot Class 31

31105	FT	31110	C	31112	CT	31113	C	31146	C	31166	C	31273	C
31405	M	31420	M	31422	M	31545		31554	C	31462	D	31468	C

LBLB   Bescot Class 37

37025	BR	37071	C	37073	FT	37087	C	37095	C	37116	0	37141	C
37142	C	37146	C	37158	C	37211	C	37212	FT	37214	FA	37240	C
37505	FT	37695	FT										

LBSB   Bescot Class 37 (Sandite Fitted)

37133	C	37154	FT	37178	F	37191	C	37196	C	37255	C	37258	C
37262	D	37330	EW	37334	F								

LCWX   Strategic Reserve Locomotives

08428		08519	0	08622		08693		08718		08731		08734	
08815		08826		08938	0	08952		20118	FR	20132	FR	20138	FR
20165	FR	20168		20169	CS	31106	C	31107	C	31119	C	31126	C
31132	FO	31134	C	31144	C	31147	C	31164	FO	31178	C	31190	C
31199	FC	31206	C	31224	C	31232	C	31235	C	31237	C	31238	C
31242	C	31270	FC	31285	C	31302	FP	31317	FO	31327	FR	31423	M
31524	C	31427		31530	C	31432		31435	C	31537	C	31538	
31546	C	31455	RR	31556	FT	37026	FD	37066	C	37088	CT	37099	C
37107	FD	37108	F	37111	FT	37156	FT	37184	C	37188	C	37201	CT
37207	C	37213	FC	37232	CT	37251	I	37423	FT	37427	EW	37431	M
37904	FS	47193	FP	47295	FP	47300	C	47308	C	47329	C	47332	C
47333	C	47334	C	47341	C	47353	C	47372	C	47478		56019	FR
56020		56037	FT	56060	FT	56114	EW						

LCXX   Stored Locomotives

08448		08586	F	08610		08619		08893	D	08901		20016	
20057		20059	FR	20066		20081		20087	BS	20092	CS	31102	C
31125	C	31128	FO	31145	C	31155	FA	31158	C	31160	F	31171	FO
31174	FC	31200	FC	31248	FO	31263	C	31301	FR	31304	FC	31312	C
31408		31411	D	31413	0	31415		31516	C	31417	D	31519	C
31526	C	31533	C	31444	C	31548	C	37078	FS	47238	FD	47357	C

LCYX   Locomotives For Withdrawal

56001 FA

LGAM   Motherwell Class 56

56056	FT	56057	EW	56058	EW	56072	FT	56079	FT	56104	FC	56123	FT
56124	FC	56128	FC	56129	FT								

LGBM   Motherwell Class 37

37043 **CT** 37069 **C** 37100 **FT** 37152 **I** 37153 **CT** 37165 **C** 37170 **C**
37175 **C** 37221 **FT** 37250 **FT** 37261 **FD** 37294 **C** 37351 **CT** 37510 **I**
37675 **FT** 37683 **FT** 37685 **I** 37692 **FC** 37693 **FT** 37702 **FT** 37712 **FP**
37714 **FS** 37796 **FS** 37797 **FC** 37799 **FT** 37801 **EW** 37802 **FT** 37893 **EW**

LGHM   Motherwell Class 37/4 (West Highland)

37401 **FT** 37403 **G** 37404 **FT** 37406 **EW** 37409 **FT** 37410 **FT** 37424 **FT**
37428 **FT** 37430 **FT**

LGML   Motherwell Class 08/09

08411   08506   08534 **D** 08561   08630   08675 **F** 08720 **D**
08735   08738 **D** 08768   08827   08881 **D** 08882   08883 **0**
08906   08910   08912   08922 **D** 09103 **D** 09202 **D** 09205 **D**

LNAK   Cardiff Canton Class 60 (South Wales)

60015 **FT** 60016 **FA** 60029 **FT** 60033 **FT** 60034 **FT** 60035 **FT** 60036 **FT**
60037 **FT** 60062 **FT** 60063 **FT** 60065 **FT** 60080 **FT** 60081 **FT** 60082 **FA**
60084 **FT** 60089 **FT** 60092 **FT** 60093 **FT** 60096 **FT**

LNBK   Cardiff Canton Class 56 (South Wales)

56010 **FT** 56018 **FT** 56032 **FS** 56040 **FT** 56044 **FT** 56052 **FT** 56053 **FT**
56064 **FT** 56073 **FT** 56076 **FS** 56103 **FT** 56113 **FT** 56115 **FT** 56119 **FT**
56121 **FC**

LNCF   Cardiff Canton Class 08/09/97

08481   08493   08576   08756 **D** 08770 **D** 08786 **D** 08798
08801   08819 **D** 08941   08953 **D** 09001   09008 **D** 09013 **D**
09015 **D** 09105 **D** 09107 **D** 09203 **D** 97806 **0**

LNCK   Cardiff Canton Class 37 (South Wales)

37411 **FT** 37412 **FT** 37416 **EW** 37701 **FT** 37704 **EW** 37887 **FT** 37889 **FT**
37894 **FC** 37895 **EW** 37896 **FT** 37897 **FT** 37898 **FT** 37899 **FC** 37901 **FT**
37902 **FS** 37903 **FS** 37905 **FS** 37906 **FT**

LNLK   Cardiff Canton Class 37 (St Blazey)

37521 **FP** 37668 **EW** 37669 **FT** 37670 **FT** 37671 **FT** 37672 **FD** 37673 **FT**
37674 **FT** 37696 **FT**

LNSK   Cardiff Canton Class 37 (Sandite Fitted)

37197 **CT** 37229 **FC** 37230 **CT** 37254 **C** 37263 **C** 37275

LNWK   Cardiff Canton Class 08 (Allied Steel & Wire)

08792   08900 **D** 08932   08942   08954 **FT** 08955   08993 **FT**
08994 **D** 08995 **FT**

LWAK   Toton Class 60 (North West)

60005 **FT** 60032 **FT** 60045 **FT** 60046 **FT** 60047 **EW** 60055 **FT** 60056 **FT**
60057 **FC** 60058 **FT** 60060 **FC** 60061 **FT** 60066 **FT** 60085 **FT** 60095 **FA**
60097 **FT**

LWBK   Immingham Class 56 (Midlands & North West)

56004   56007 FT 56022 FT 56025 FT 56029 F 56033 FT 56036 CT
56047 CT 56049 CT 56054 FT 56059 FA 56066 FT 56070 FT 56071 FT
56086 FT 56092 FT 56093 FT 56096 EW 56099 FT 56101 FT 56105 EW
56125 FT 56127 FT 56132 FT 56133 FT

LWCW   Springs Branch Class 37 (North West)

37405 M 37407 FT 37413 FT 37415 EW 37419 EW 37426 M 37509 FT
37518 FS 37520 FS

LWMC   Crewe Diesel Class 37/4 (North West Passenger)

37402 F 37408 BR 37414 RR 37417 F 37418 EW 37420 RR 37421 RR
37422 RR 37425 RR 37429 RR

LWNW   Springs Branch Class 31 (North West)

31130 FC 31142 C 31154 C 31163 C 31185 C 31188 C 31201 FC
31203 C 31207 C 31229 C 31233 C 31255 C 31275 FC 31306 C
31319 FC 31410 RR 31512 C 31514 C 31421 RR 31434   31439 RR
31450   31465 RR 31467

LWSP   Springs Branch Class 08

08397 F 08485   08489 F 08676   08817 BS 08867 O 08884
08894   08911 D 08915 F 08918 D 08925

CARRIAGE & TRACTION CO.

PWLO   Crewe Diesel Class 47

47710 W 47712 W

PWLS   Crewe Diesel Class 47 (Stored)

47488 W 47701 RX 47703 W 47705 W 47709 RX

EW&S (FORMERLY RES)

PXLB   Crewe Diesel Class 47 (Extended Range)

47721 RX 47722 RX 47725 RX 47726 RX 47727 RX 47732 RX 47733 RX
47734 RX 47736 RX 47737 RX 47738 RX 47739 RX 47741 RX 47742 RX
47744 RX 47745 RX 47746 RX 47747 RX 47749 RX 47750 RX 47756 RX
47757 RX 47758 RX 47759 RX 47760 RX 47761 RX 47762 RX 47763 RX
47764 RX 47765 RX 47766 RX 47767 RX 47768 RX 47769 RX 47770 RX
47771 RX 47772 RX 47773 RX 47774 RX 47775 RX 47776 RX 47777 RX
47778 RX 47779 RX 47780 RX 47781 RX 47782 RX 47783 RX 47784 RX
47785 RX 47786 RX 47787 RX 47788 RX 47789 RX 47790 RX 47791 RX
47792 RX 47793 RX

PXLC   Crewe Diesel Class 47

47492 RX 47565 RX 47572 R 47575 R 47584 RX 47596 RX 47624 RX
47627 RX 47628 RX 47634 R 47635 R 47640 R

PXLD   Crewe Diesel Class 47 (Reserve/Stored)

47467 **BR** 47475 **RX** 47501 **R** 47513 **BR** 47519 **G** 47520 **I** 47523 **M**
47524 **RX** 47528 **M** 47530 **RX** 47532 **RX** 47535 **RX** 47536 **RX** 47566 **RX**
47576 **RX** 47704 **RX** 47715 **N** 47716 **RX** 47972 **CS**

PXLE   Crewe Electric Class 86/90

86208 **I** 86210 **RX** 86241 **RX** 86243 **RX** 86254 **RX** 86261 **RX** 86401 **RX**
86416 **RX** 86417 **RX** 86419 **RX** 86424 **RX** 86425 **RX** 86426 **RX** 86430 **RX**
90016 **RX** 90017 **RX** 90018 **RX** 90019 **RX** 90020 **RX**

PXLH   Crewe Diesel Class 47 (75 mph maximum)

47474 **R** 47489 **R** 47522 **R**

PXLK   Crewe Diesel Class 47/9

47971 **BR** 47976 **C**

PXLP   Crewe Diesel Class 47 (VIP Fleet)

47798 **0** 47799 **0**

PXLS   Crewe Diesel/Heaton/Willesden Class 08

08578 **R** 08599   08633 **RX** 08635   08685   08701 **RX** 08702
08711 **RX** 08714 **RX** 08742 **RX** 08757 **RX** 08802 **RX** 08804   08873 **RX**
08890 **D** 08896   08897 **D** 08919 **RX** 08921 **EW**

PXLT   Crewe Diesel Class 08

08402 **D** 08594   08695   08865

PXXA   Locomotives For Withdrawal

08647 **G** 08668   08818   47471 **IO** 47481 **BR** 47539 **RX** 47547 **N**
47717 **R**

WESTERN TRACK RENEWALS

RNRG   Reading Class 97/6

97651 **0** 97654 **0**

EVERSHOLT LEASING

SAXL   Locomotives Off Lease

86103 **I** 86213 **I** 86219 **I** 86249 **I**

RACAL-BRT

TAKB   Bescot Class 20

20075 **T** 20128 **T** 20131 **T** 20187 **T**

TAKX   Stored Locomotives

20007   20032   20072   20104 **FR** 20117   20121   20190
20215 **FR**

PRIVATELY OWNED LOCOS

XHSD   Direct Rail Services Class 20/3

20301 **0**   20302 **0**   20303 **0**   20304 **0**   20305 **0**

XYPA   ARC Class 59/1

59101 **0**   59102 **0**   59103 **0**   59104 **0**

XYPD   Hunslet Barclay Class 20/9

20901 **0**   20902 **0**   20903 **0**   20904 **0**   20905 **0**   20906 **0**

XYPN   National Power Class 59/2

59201 **0**   59202 **0**   59203 **0**   59204 **0**   59205 **0**   59206 **0**

XYPO   Foster Yeoman Class 59/0

59001 **0**   59002 **0**   59003 **0**   59004 **0**   59005 **0**

PRESERVED LOCOMOTIVES OF BRITISH RAILWAYS 9th edition

Peter Hall & Peter Fox.

The complete guide to all remaining Ex-British Railways and Constituent Companies, steam, diesel & electric locomotives, and diesel & electric multiple units. For the first time this popular volume now includes locomotives & multiple units of London Underground Limited and its predecessors, plus expanded coverage of locomotives once owned by the British Military. Also includes a full list of preservation sites and industrial locations. A5 size. Thread Sewn. Illustrated in colour and black & white. **£7.95**.

PRESERVED COACHING STOCK OF BRITISH RAILWAYS

Part 1 - BR Design Stock. £7.95
Part 2 - Pre-Nationalisation Stock. £8.95

Peter Hall & Peter Fox.

The ideal companions to 'Preserved Locomotives of British Railways' are now available. Part One contains full details of all BR Design Coaching Stock together with Pullman cars from the same era. Background information and brief design details are included, plus all numbers carried and current locations for every vehicle. A complete BR hauled coaching stock lot number list is also provided. This is the first time such a listing has been published in the clear Platform 5 format which also includes a full index to preservation sites including OS grid references.

Part Two is now available. This volume lists all coaching stock vehicles designed between the 1923 grouping and nationalisation in 1948, which are known to be still in existence. Details of number, former number(s), current location and usage (where appropriate), are included for every vehicle, plus technical data for each class of vehicle. The informative narrative and explanatory notes from the authors make this book a must for all followers of Railway Preservation and coaching stock.

LIVERY CODES

Locomotives are blue unless otherwise indicated. The colour of the lower half of the bodyside is stated first. Minor variations to these liveries are ignored.

BR   Revised blue (large numbers and full height BR logo).

BS   Blue with red solebar stripe.

C   Civil Engineers (grey and yellow).

CS   Central services (grey and red).

CT   Civil Engineers livery with Transrail markings.

D   Departmental (plain grey with black cab doors).

E   Eurostar (GB) locomotive livery - As 'F' with blue roof and cast Channel Tunnel logo.

EW English, Welsh & Scottish Railway Ltd. (maroon with large maroon EW&S lettering and number on broad gold band between cabs).

F   New Railfreight (two-tone grey sides with sub-sector markings).

FA   Trainload Construction - As 'F' with construction markings (blue blocks on a yellow background).

FC   Trainload Coal - As 'F' with coal markings (black diamonds on a yellow background).

FD   Old Railfreight Distribution - As 'F' with Railfreight Distribution markings (red diamonds on a yellow background).

FL   New Railfreight Livery with Loadhaul lettering.

FE   New Railfreight Distribution - Two-tone grey with blue roof and Railfreight Distribution lettering and markings (red diamonds on a yellow background).

FF   Freightliner - As 'F' with Freightliner lettering and markings (red diagonal stripes behind right hand cab door).

FM New Railfreight Livery with Mainline markings.

FO   Old Railfreight (grey sides, yellow cabsides and full height BR logo).

FP   Trainload Petroleum - As 'F' with Trainload Petroleum markings (blue waves on a yellow background).

FR   As 'FO' but with a red solebar stripe and a slightly smaller BR logo.

FS   Trainload Metals - As 'F' with metals markings (blue chevrons on a yellow background).

FT   New Railfreight Livery with Transrail markings (large white 'T' on a blue circle with a red outline underlined with red stripes).

G   BR or GWR green.

GE   Gatwick Express (white and dark grey with claret stripe and Gatwick Express lettering and motif).

GN   Great North Eastern Railway (dark blue with an orange bodyside stripe and gold GNER lettering).

GW   Great Western Trains (green and ivory with Great Western Trains logo and lettering).

     InterCity (white and dark grey with red stripe and swallow motif).

IO   Old InterCity (light grey and dark grey with red stripe, yellow lower cab sides and BR logo).

H   Loadhaul (black with orange cabsides and Loadhaul lettering).

M   Mainline (as old 'IO' but without the yellow lower cabsides and BR logo).

MD Merseyrail Departmental (dark grey and yellow with Merseyrail logo and lettering).

ML   Mainline Freight (blue with silver body stripe and Mainline markings).
N   Network SouthEast (grey/white/red/white/blue/white).
O   Other livery (non-standard - refer to text).
PL   Porterbrook Leasing (purple at one end, white at the other with small logo and lettering behind the left-hand cab doors. The livery represents an enlarged portion of the Porterbrook logo with the colours reversed on the other side).
R   Parcels (post office red and dark grey).
RR   Regional Railways (grey/light blue/white/dark blue).
RX   Rail express systems (post office red with Res blue & black markings)
SC   Stagecoach (grey/orange/red/white/blue/white).
T   Racal-BRT (two-tone grey with green markings).
U   Grey undercoat. Certain locos emerged in undercoat whilst E,W & S and Great Western Trains were deciding on a livery to adopt as standard.
W   Waterman Railways (black with cream & red lining).